You Will Find Your People

How to Make Meaningful
Friendships as an Adult

LANE MOORE

Abrams Image, New York

Editor: Samantha Weiner
Designer: Zach Bokhour
Managing Editor: Glenn Ramirez
Production Manager: Anet Sirna-Bruder

Library of Congress Control Number: 2022948254

ISBN: 978–1-4197–6256–7
eISBN: 978–1-64700–714–0

Printed and bound in the United States

10 9 8 7 6 5 4 3 2 1

Many names and identifying details have been changed.

Abrams Image books are available at special discounts when purchased in quantity for premiums and promotions as well as fundraising or educational use. Special editions can also be created to specification. For details, contact specialsales@abramsbooks.com or the address below.

Abrams Image® is a registered trademark of Harry N. Abrams, Inc.

ABRAMS The Art of Books
195 Broadway, New York, NY 10007
abramsbooks.com

This book is for anyone who hasn't found their people yet, in the ways they've always hoped for. May this be a guide for you to figure out who you are, and who you need, so you can finally have the chosen family we all deserve.

This book is dedicated to Lights, who despite being eight pounds and a dog, taught me what real friendship looks like.

Contents

How To Make Friends

Ilana: Dude, I would follow you into hell, brother!
Abbi: I would take you on my shoulders, like, I'd strap
you up, and I'd be like let's go to hell. —*Broad City*

I really thought I'd have friends by now. Don't get me wrong,
I have people I talk to who I really like. I have people I laugh
with and see once every six months, people who text me and
say we should do something soon, and we might even make
plans, but then we each hope the other will cancel because
we're both tired. I have those, yes. But I really thought I'd have
friends by now, in the way I understood friendship to mean as
a child.

My earliest memories from childhood are watching, in
awe, the depictions of tight-knit friend groups in TV and
movies. I'd watch them excitedly on-screen, as though it was
a fortune teller showing me a glimpse into my future great-
friend-having life. I always assumed that even if I didn't have
the friendships that I saw on TV at that very moment, once
I became an adult, they would surely materialize. And maybe
you did too.

We all hoped we'd find them in early childhood: soulmate
best friends born next door to you, just months apart. And if

not then, we'd find them in middle school, or in high school. And then we'll know them for the rest of our lives. And if that doesn't work out, everyone always says you get to reinvent yourself in college and find your people there. Yeah!

But then we get to high school. And then to college. Or we don't go to college. Or we kept to ourselves in college. Or we experienced trauma during that time. Or the friend-ships we found didn't turn out the way we'd hoped. And even when they did, even in the best-case scenarios, people change, people leave. We might not keep in touch. We might move, they might move. And those friendships become crystallized in our memory, revived only by an occasional Google search to see that *Wow, Alison still works at the mall? And she has a KID?* We might still talk to them in our heads, hoping they will get the messages, but knowing they won't. And being mostly OK with that.

No one tells you that the ages of eighteen to twenty-two are pretty much prime friendship real estate. That's *it*. You're around the largest group of people your age that you'll ever be around in your life, who are all very eager to create their friend groups. That's your shot. So you'd better have a "normal" college experience and the good fortune to be ready and able to meet your friend group exactly at that time, or else you'll get lost in the over-twenty-two hellscape that is "How the hell do I make a friend now?"

It can often feel like a cruel game of musical chairs that started years ago, and we didn't even know it had started, let alone that it was (seemingly) about to end.

In elementary school I learned most of what I knew about friendships from TV, and TV had assured me that everyone got between one and six best friends. They were guaranteed, and maybe I just had to wait a little longer until the cruel politics of high school subsided to find them. And I knew exactly what to look for when that happened. The types of best friends everyone in pop culture seems to get:

- Your steadfast, biggest-fan best friend who is always there to be extremely silly with you and remind you how incredible you are. They are kind and empathetic and the one person who always shows up with soup if you experience even the slightest disappointment.
- The coworker you don't really see outside of work, but when you're at work, you leave thoughtful snacks on each other's desks.
- The "wild" friend who is more adventurous and reckless than you are and pushes you to expand the limits of who you think you can be, or if you're the wild friend, the more reserved friend who you're constantly encouraging to push the limits of who they think they can be.
- The "wow I didn't expect this friendship to blossom the way it did and yet here we are" friend you didn't see coming, and it was the best surprise of your whole life.

And a bunch of other ancillary friends we're told will be fun to hang out with for a while at least, lighting up your teens and twenties like a well-ornamented "these are my PEOPLE!" tree, shedding leaves painlessly as needed. No painful friend breakups, no falling-outs, no heartbreak, just brief cameos that drift away with ease and everyone is still whole afterward.

I needed all these types of friends, because society told me I did, so I clung to the people I met who even remotely fit these descriptions like hard-won Girl Scout badges, no matter how unhealthy the dynamic was, as proof I could do it. I could be just like everyone else in this one way, since I couldn't be like everyone else who had perfect families. (Please see my first book: *How to Be Alone.*) That was very much out of my hands. But friendships? I could do that. Contort myself to make a bunch of people like me and never leave? Can't wait! There's no way you could go wrong when that is your very upsetting view of friendship!

Perhaps this was a self-fulfilling prophecy: Because this is what I thought friendship was, it always devolved into nightmare territory. As close as I'd get to having a best friend, the relationships were always short-lived. No matter how promising the beginning was, something would invariably throw a wrench into the intimacy I'd craved so deeply and needed like air. My junior high best friend decided we were both acting "too into each other" (we were into each other), so she ended the friendship. My high school best friend's family moved far away, and I grieved the loss of her like a death. Replace, repeat, and never stop trying and then grieving, trying and then grieving.

If you've survived a Greek myth–esque series of relational disappointments, you know that trying to figure out how to make a friend when you've been hurt so many times, or never really felt loved or accepted in a lasting way, or never had a model of healthy friendship, can feel impossible.

My definition of healthy friendship is personal to me, as it is to us all. So there may be stories I tell where someone did something to me that broke my heart, that you wouldn't think twice about, no big deal, or where I react to someone in a way that feels foreign to you. Because we are all a unique combination of needs, and past hurts, and what we did or didn't get as children, which directly informs what we need now, and what we're able to tolerate, for better or worse.

Most friendships aren't comprised of one person who is bad and one who is good, one who is wrong and one who is right. They're comprised of people who are either a good match for each other or they are not. Above all, your friendships should allow you to feel safe and to feel seen, and do whatever is required to make you feel that way, and if a person can't or won't do that for you, you are absolutely allowed to walk away. Perhaps without judgment, without an indictment that they're bad, but resolute in the knowledge that you deserve to have whatever you need to have.

My childhood had lacked consistency, so it's extremely important for me to have people in my life who do everything they say they will do. Because I lacked that foundation as a child, having people in my life who show me that reliability is crucial; it's what I need, and it's valid. It's also valid for someone to not be able to provide any consistency for themselves or anyone else, perhaps because of their own experiences. But we will probably not be forming a tight bond with each other any time soon, as it would be hell for us both: I'd constantly be disappointed, and they'd constantly feel disappointing. No thank you.

Friendships require so much timing, luck, communication, and puzzle-piece compatibility that any two people who make it to the promised land of true friendship are almost heroic. I'm sure some friendships coast and get there, drifting like a bottle thrown into the ocean and finally reaching land. But I think, more often, friendships are little ships set out to sea, with two people on board who've never been in a boat like this, and have only passive knowledge of sailing, trying to steer it and keep it afloat, and have fun along the way. And then one day you see the shore, and you decide, together, to row and steer, taking turns in whatever way feels best for you both, until you get to that shore and you're there, finally. And then you'll go out into different oceans, of course, over the course of your lives together. But now you know how to divide up tasks, how to best work together, and you're not as worried someone is going to jump ship and hop into another boat that seems easier, or more fun. You've made a choice to be in this one, to take care of it, to take it where it deserves to go. That takes so much trust and intimacy and again, above all, choosing each other.

But we don't teach people how to do this, how to create friendships, how to nurture them, how to choose better, and then when and how to end them if they're not working. And because of that, so many of us are just fumbling around, hoping one day we'll stumble into the friendships of our dreams because we want them, because we deserve them.

How do you find a healthy friendship when it's something you've never experienced yet? And even if you were finally offered it, how do you recognize it and find the courage to accept it? How are those of us who have been wounded or traumatized supposed to find healthy friendships if we were shown at a formative age that we didn't deserve them?

We don't know the answer, but god, we fight for it. We want to connect so much that we keep putting money in the friendship slot machine, hoping for a different outcome, no matter how much we continue to lose. Because we know if we win, we win big. We'll get friends who will let us fall apart around them, who we can be ourselves with, and who will accept all parts of us, no matter how messy and fractured some of those parts might be.

As heavy as it is, I believe that it is worth carrying the baggage of our past, taking it with us to each new person, even though we worry they're going to see it and ask why there's so much stuff. Sometimes we pick up even *more* baggage with every person we meet; things they give to us that we didn't want, didn't need, but they are ours now. And sometimes we have so many bags that it seems too burdensome to try again, too heavy a weight to carry.

But we do try again. We learn to pack better, we learn where to bury things, where to set things free, what we can throw away, what we can sew back together.

One of the biggest things everyone seems to stress about in their day-to-day life is their friendships:

Are they being a jerk?
Am I the jerk?
I said this to them, was that too much?
They said this, what did they mean by that?
Is this toxic?
Are they mad at me?
Am I mad at them?
How do I make this better? Is it possible?

After years of searching and waiting and hoping and being disappointed, I wanted to know if it's possible to have the friends we dream of. We hear stories like that all the time, that someone has incredible friends, just incredible. And we believe it, because if very bad things can exist, very good things can exist just as well.

So why couldn't that happen to you? Or to me?

I used to think I was the only one struggling with this,

that everyone else had their friendships fully sorted, and that I was the only kid who wasn't picked for kickball, wondering why I hadn't gotten it right yet.

But I know from meeting so many people who tell me they're on the same path, that I'm not the only one out there who has struggled to find their people. I'm not the only one who is doing the heavy work to figure out who they are, what they want, and how to spot the roadblocks in front of them that they truly can't wait to knock out of the way, with explosives if need be. I'm not the only one with harmful patterns they are so exhausted, and honestly even bored, by. I'm not the only one who is so unbelievably tired of complaining about frustrating friends, and genuinely ecstatic at the idea of having friendships that *just work*. Just pure and simple "They liked me, I liked them, and it *just worked*." Then you get to be one of those people who say things like "And we've been friends ever since."

I know that often when life has been its most challenging, its most painful, its most hopeless, that is when something really good happens. And I also know, and hopefully you do too, that as I've done the (grueling, it is in fact often grueling) work on myself, as each friendship ended, I was in a better place to be able to choose a better friend the next time. (And then sometimes you unknowingly slide backward into your old patterns, like way too far backward, and you're like wait, how did my Friendship GPS break so badly?!) It's all a refinement process. The more you know about yourself and your patterns, the better equipped you are to home in on what you truly want and need from your friends, and to know how to spot it. So why can't we find the courage to start taking greater leaps forward, now that we know better?

But even once you know better, it can still feel like it's impossible to make friends with anyone after you're out of high school or college. Without the built-in system of "a bunch of people in a building who you have to talk to sometimes," the entire world can feel like an awkward bar you just want to leave.

And even if you ask someone how to do it, most people just tell you, "Join a club!" or "Join a gym!" But if you're like me and you have no idea what kind of club you would join (a club for people obsessed with watching the same TV show over and over again? Those people are at home watching the same TV show over and over again) and either you already belong to a gym and you go there to exercise quietly and then leave, or you just really, really don't want to join a gym, here are some places to start:

1. **Message someone you constantly interact with online.** If you're on social media or in any groups online, odds are you have someone who always replies to you, sends you messages, or likes all your posts. These are a lot of subtle interactions that could easily turn into "dude, we should be friends maybe?" messages. So why not try?

2. **Write to a mutual friend who you've always felt like you'd get along with.** You already have your friend in common, so it's worth it to see if you'd get along when it's just the two of you. I once knew a guy who had really cool friends, but honestly I was not that into the guy himself. One day, I ran into some of his friends on the subway and it turns out they all thought I was really awesome and also didn't like that other guy. It was a beautiful moment.

3. **Go to cool shows or restaurants alone.** I can't tell you how often I've heard people tell me they came to my comedy shows by themselves and met really cool people they became friends with. And if the idea of this terrifies you, it's so helpful to see this less as "Oh no, I'm gonna look like a loser who is alone" and more like "What if I meet another cool person who is also there alone and we bond, and because I went alone, I created space for that to happen?"

4. **Make plans outside of work with that coworker who you think is cool.** I once worked with a woman who was basically my best friend in the office and then, one day, it dawned on me: Who says she couldn't be my best friend in general? And lucky for me, she was just as hilarious and fun outside of work, if not more so.

5. **Reach out to someone you only see in drinking situations to do something non-drinking during the day.** Cool Drunk Sara is also probably Cool Sober Sara Who Loves Getting Tapas After Work. You won't know until you try.

6. **Invite your friends' significant others to stuff.** This can be touchy depending on the situation, so obviously don't do this if you know it could pose a problem, but if you think your friend's girlfriend is really cool and there's a possible friendship there, go for it and see if you're right.

7. **Go to a dog park.** Dog or not, dog parks are such great ways to meet other really friendly people (well, mostly, sometimes there is someone there who is such a dick and you're like, "Why are you bringing this energy to such a holy place? Why?") and worst case, you get to play with dogs. But in general, dogs are such a great icebreaker.

When I'm with my dog, I meet multiple people every day who are extremely kind and cool to chat with. We might not become best friends just because our dogs played together for ten minutes, but it can satisfy that need for connection in a really beautiful way.

8. **Try putting more effort into the friendships you have.** It can be easy to think your current friends aren't good enough for you or not giving you the things you want in the relationship and you should find new people, and sometimes that's true. But before you go off thinking it's not you, it's them (which it might be!), try reaching out, and communicating, and putting some more effort in and see if that helps things.

9. **Encourage yourself to make/keep plans with your friends, even though sitting inside alone watching friendships on TV seems way better.** Sometimes you genuinely need to recharge and reschedule, which I fully encourage, but other times I need to remind myself to actually keep plans and take a chance that this might be exactly what I needed, even if solitude seems safer. And then I come home feeling so happy that I took the risk and left my cocoon for a bit.

Does all of this take more effort than sitting there waiting for your dream friends to show up like UPS packages? Yes. Is that scary because there might be rejection or disappointment? Yes. But often the only way for things to be different is for us to start doing things differently, and putting all that we're learning into practice. So many of us are working so hard on ourselves; we're going to therapy, we're reading books on attachment and trauma and connection (I mean, hi, you're

11

right here, good job). Since I was a kid I have wanted to untangle all of these knots, wound up like shitty headphones, so I can just lay in the grass and listen to a song I really love. And yes, it is frustrating to get those knots out, and yes, you can want to give up, and you do give up sometimes. But once we untangle them, bit by bit, that's when we get to move on to joy. And maybe we'll remember how hard it was to untangle the knots, but I think, more than anything, we will be more preoccupied with how happy we are with what we have now that we did the work.

Well, unless you're pretty sure you don't deserve friendship and love. And in that case, let me gently affirm.

You deserve to have friendships in which the conversation is easy, and you feel seen. You deserve to have those days where you get in the car, and you pick that person up, or they pick you up, and they got you a coffee exactly the way you like it, *aw thanks*. You deserve to pick up ice cream on the way because *oh man that place looks so good, you wanna stop?* And sing along to whatever's on the radio, one hand out the window. And that is all it is. No asterisks, no fine print, just purely good.

You deserve to have friendships where there's an equal give and take. Friends who understand you, and you have FUN, true, silly little kid fun (even if, and especially if, you never got to truly have fun as a kid, because you were already basically an adult). Friends who allow and encourage you to have healthy boundaries, as they work to establish their own.

And then maybe what happens next isn't tragic this time. Maybe it's just good, forever and ever. At last.

Figuring Out What Kinds of Friendships You Want

Romy: I think you are, like, the funnest person I know.
Michele: Me too, with you!
—*Romy and Michele's High School Reunion*

Sometimes I see people on the Internet say things like, "I see you all talk about your friends and they're so bad, and it made me realize how grateful I am to have great friends from when I was little. You all need to get better friends." And I want to scream, "We want to, bro, BUT WHERE?"

We can never say these things though. Lest we be perceived as bitter or whiny or negative, we can't speak about the fact that many of us are rightly a little upset that we didn't get that. Because from the time we started to watch TV, or read books, or watch movies, we have been told that everyone is destined to have a friend they met in an adorable way when they were six years old and, for better or worse (mostly better, we're told), you will know them until you die.

I can't tell you how much I wanted that. And as the years passed, and I became fifteen, sixteen, seventeen years old, and beyond, and noticed ... *uh-oh*. I think I missed the deadline and I'm not sure where the sign-up sheet is. How do I speak to the manager of friendships? I won't yell, but I have some questions. Where are mine? Did I not spell my name correctly?

I wanted the thing that Drew Barrymore promised us in one interview I read as a kid: a chosen family.

A chosen family involved enough people so if things weren't working out with one of them, you had another three to five people you could go to, who would be there for you. And the group dynamic would also make all your friendships ultimately unshakeable, because if anything happened within the group, if any discord occurred, there was always someone there to say, "Hey, everyone! Stop fighting. Let's all help you see this clearly and repair it." Even just writing that, I had a wave of serotonin because, can you even imagine?

It will not surprise you to know that it did not occur exactly like that for me. Nor did it for most of us.

For the majority of the last ten years or so, many of us have spent most of our friendships talking to each other through text. So when I watch TV, I immediately zero in on interactions where, if they were like real life usually is, the whole scene would just be these people texting, but screenwriters put them in the same room instead. The thinking being that just showing two people texting is not interesting to show on TV, there's no movement, no intimacy, and it's boring to watch. And they're right! All of those things are true, yet that's what we do in real life anyway.

There are so many examples of friendships in movies and TV shows that are unrealistic to many of us, which might make you feel a little ripped off when you grow up and realize, "Oh wow, it is very rarely like that?" Unrealistic as they may be, here are several friendship tropes that I still want to believe are possible, because that would rule:

1. **"Friends always do exactly what they say they'll do!"** And if they ever let you down, it only happens once and there's a whole episode devoted to them realizing they really hurt you, and then they surprise you with approximately nineteen cakes and a trip to Italy. Instead of doing simply nothing.

2. **"Friends always know what you need and freely give it to you, even if you never tell them!"** Every one of your friends will always go to the ends of the earth for you, fight for you, and show up for you in exactly the way you need it, even if you're unable to articulate what you need. Sounds convenient to me!

3. **"Friends champion your dreams and actively help you achieve them!"** Even if you're in entirely different career fields, your friends still somehow introduce you to all the right people to help you achieve your dreams, re-route you when you're frustrated, and generally make sure you're always doing everything you should be doing, like little unpaid life coaches. That's a thing that exists? Where?!

4. **"Your friends constantly push you to be the best person you can be!"** Somehow they know what the ideal version of you is and they help you to be that. Seriously, would love to get a rush shipment on this one.

5. **"Your best friend will be your total opposite in every way and yet this will be very fun and easy somehow!"** So my best friend and I have only one thing in common and it's that we like each other? Hm, that sounds ripe for arguments and differences in how we'll give and receive love? Right? No? OK, I believe you, never mind!

6. **"They probably introduce you to your spouse, and it is probably their hot brother!"** Still waiting on this. My

friends' siblings do not casually look like Chris Evans and/or are already married. A disappointment.

7. **"If your friends live far away, you know it is only temporary and you will live in the same city one day and you will have one misunderstanding max and you'll be fine."** You will definitely never feel lonely at all, nor will you be unable to stop wondering when you'll live in the same city so you can actually have friends who live nearby.

8. **"You will never fight ever."** And if you do, it will be once in your life and bring you closer. And if you fight more often than that, yours isn't a healthy friendship. (While this can be true to some degree, that can also be a recipe for "things we never talk about that will one day result in friendship divorce.")

9. **"You will meet all your friends when you're little kids and it's always great and you die in matching graves!"** I still want this. I feel it might be too late, due to the fact that I'm an adult and have no remaining childhood friends, but I remain hopeful.

10. **"Your friend hears you broke up with your partner, and they race over!"** The "You went through (insert anything uncomfortable at all) and I immediately dropped any plans I had to physically race over to you with gifts and/or support," is the one that kills me the most. We see this trope so often in the media, and I have literally never had that happen in my life. And I have needed it so many times, for so many things more dire than a simple, clean-cut breakup.

To be fair, the idea of most people being able to put together an impromptu "I wanted to cheer you up, so everyone in our friend group put together an elaborate $2,000+ surprise party for you because you're struggling at your new job!" feels laughable.

I love *New Girl* dearly, and one of my favorite moments is when Schmidt worries he has bad taste in things, so the group buys him an extremely expensive chair and surprises him with it at his house. Reagan says, "Happy birthday, Schmidt!" and Nick says something along the lines of, "It's not his birthday. We just do things like this, I don't understand it either." Taking that moment to recognize that TV shows are actively showing people what friendship looks like—lavish gifts, everyone in the group always available at the exact same times, being down to help each other through life's most mundane inconveniences—when that is not most people's experience whatsoever was really refreshing. It seems so rare to see a television show acknowledge that the closeness and consistency of these friendships isn't always what we get in real life, despite how much we may want them.

And we rightly want everything we've read about and watched for years, all of the types of close-knit friends we've come to love in fiction, we want that for ourselves so much. I've boiled these down to four friendship archetypes that I grew up aspiring to and continue to aspire to:

1. **Casual Friends:** These are people you see sometimes, and you're always happy to see them, but the relationship never really progresses past this—and it's fine because neither of you really needs to. You're more than happy to run into them at a bar and be like "Ayyy, I've seen your face and body before and I know your name! Look at US!" (Note: I never really aspired to have casual friends, since I usually

wanted those to become closer friends as well, because I have no chill.)

2. **Friends:** This obviously can mean many things to many people, but for the sake of this argument, let's say this is someone you've hung out with more than a few times and shared some very real moments with, moments that felt deeper to you than those shared with a casual friend. Because that's really where these differences lie: how close you feel to them, and how close they feel to you. It's all subjective, but this is that middle ground of "We talk sometimes, I would help them if they needed me, but I probably wouldn't drop everything to take them to a doctor's appointment they were antsy about, and would instead send supportive texts."

3. **The Friend Group:** Oh, how I have longed for a group of friends where we all get along and become a tight-knit family and all look very cool and are always available at the same times. Each one with a distinct personality, so you have a sort of tasting menu, a wine flight if you will, of people you can go to at any moment to meet even your most superficial needs. Need a friend to hack into the security mainframe during your espionage? Great, call up your hacker friend who's great with gadgets, of course! You're getting married? Your world-class chef friend will of course be making all of the food for free!

4. **Best Friend:** Again, could mean lots of things, but my personal definition is someone who you can talk with regularly and call at any time, about anything, and be any way with. Totally guard-down, open communication of boundaries and feelings, you're both down for all of it, forever, you're fully IN. Whatever they need, they've got

you. You talk all the time, pretty constantly, and you're basically two halves of the same person.

I don't know many people who have all of these at all times, but let's look at the pros and cons of each.

a. **Casual Friends**
   Pros: Getting to feel like a cool mob boss everywhere you go in town. "Yeah I know him, we go way back." This is such a state of being, I'm getting chills just thinking about it.
   Cons: You might struggle with having too many casual friends and end up feeling weirdly alone because no one really knows you, and you never really feel fully seen and part of any one community.

b. **Friends**
   See "this entire book" for further definitions of pros and cons.

c. **The Friend Group**
   Pros: Potentially multiple closets to pick from on any given day. The ability to have multiple people to go to when something is going on with you, or something is going on with two of you. There's a higher probability that one of them will be able to show up for you and rally to make sure you're always taken care of, and always have backup. I'm drooling as I write this.
   Cons: Where do I begin? Shared calendars to schedule outings, unless you live in a *Sex and the City* episode where they seemingly just knew which hot restaurant to show up at every single day, at the same time, and all before the invention of a group chat. There's also the danger of

people pairing off, depending on the number of people in the friend group, and being the odd one out. Or not being as close with some, as you are with others. Or people taking sides in a fight.

There is truly so much potential for this to become a mess, and it can be a ton of scheduling and work, but I still want it. It just seems so rare that I often don't even think of it as a possibility for myself. Not because I wouldn't love a friend group, not even because a friend group seems like so much more work, which it absolutely does. But because having one just seems like winning the lottery. Ah, but she is elusive.

d. The Best Friend

Pros: You get to have the friend you are closer to than anyone else. You tell them everything first, you want to do everything together, your penultimate plus-one. Your emergency contact, no question. The One.

Let's take a second here to really go into what it means to have a Best Friend, and the ease, or lack thereof, in finding said Best Friend.

Trying to find The One can be challenging as hell. Since I was a kid, I've treated any friendship like it could be The One, and would invest everything I had into it, especially if it seemed like the other person was doing the same. I was always on the lookout for this, in the same way we're taught to always be on the lookout for romantic relationships. And it's fairly similar to one in that the feeling has to be mutual, and you need to know it means the same thing to both of you. I know a lot of people have no issue with calling twenty people their best friend. But I had long seen it as a fairly cut-and-dried thing: "There is my best friend, who is my other half, and then there's the rest of my friends, who are also good too. But they're not THE BEST! That's just Sheila, and Sheila only." (Please note: I do not currently know any Sheilas. Maybe that's the problem. Must meet more Sheilas.)

Instead of "dating around" for friends, the way other people might, I would just find one person I had a connection with and ride that wave until it crashed. And I either drowned or realized they knew how to surf and I didn't. I have always gone all in with anyone I've ever gotten close to. And this is a beautiful thing that is not always in my best interest. I think it's lovely to be invested and hopeful and devoted and go all in, but just like water, it can either nourish you or kill you.

This was something that always made me feel different from other people, who seemed to treat friendships like they were hair ties on their wrists that had somehow fallen off. You probably have a million of them at home, they're cheap, replaceable, no big deal. To me, friendships were very expensive earrings I'd saved up for, so if I lost one, or *gasp* both, how would I ever replace them? So I would check my ears multiple times a day, grateful and protective of this valuable thing that was so hard won, and so very precious.

One of my favorite quotes, from actress/writer Jen Richards, puts it so well: "I rarely meet men in real life as extraordinary as ones on film, and rarely see women on film as extraordinary as ones I know in real life."

Similarly, I have rarely experienced a friend group in real life as wonderful as the ones I've seen on film and rarely seen friends on-screen ebb and flow in their ability to meet your needs, as the friends I've known in real life. The hard thing is, TV and movies began as a form of escapism, but we don't look to either for purely that anymore, and we haven't for a long time. We look to them to know how to act, to know how to connect, to know what friendships should look like.

So when we look around and our Best Friend Forever hasn't materialized, nor has our core friend group of four people who all know each other and all represent distinct qualities and personalities that magically work together, forming a mini coven that gets lunch together every day at three P.M., hasn't found us yet, we feel like we've failed.

I want my One Person (more, if available), or at least to know who my people were and how they worked, like a friendship Swiss Army knife. I want to have my regular thing I always order, if that order was a person. I want to know that if I am having a problem at work, I call this person. If I am struggling with health issues, I call this person. If I am having a problem with anything at all, I call this person. I want a toolbox, and I want to know and trust my tools. I want to know exactly what kind of wrench I need for each repair, and I want them to be there when I reach for them. And I know they're people, I know. But I want the certainty I'd assumed I would have by now. To be able to dial a number, and know they'll pick up. To be able to text someone something and have them know exactly what I need at that moment. To have someone do everything in their power to prop me up, just as much as I do them. Someone to walk through life with.

And the shame of not being able to achieve that yet sets in and creeps through any previous cracks we already had from the shame that came before. "Because I don't deserve it," we think. "That makes sense." We talk so openly, so freely, about body shame, as we rightly should, but we don't talk about the shame that comes from constantly seeing other people having loving, consistent, reliable friendships as though everyone has that and if you don't, that's super weird, what's wrong with you? That relational shame.

What does it say about you that you couldn't easily find four to five people who all understand you constantly, make you feel seen, anticipate every possible need, and try at all costs to protect you from experiencing pain? And if someone caused you to feel pain, why didn't they swoop in and hold you while you cried for days, which is always what happens to everyone of course. Why couldn't you find that, so easily, at the local corner store, like everyone else on earth did, you genuine freak?

You couldn't find people who were basically trauma therapists, with deep wells of empathy and compassion, who always understood how race, gender, and class have affected you personally? WHY??? Fix that.

But the trouble is, this is one part of life we can't simply fix by going out and choosing to, because finding friends—real, true friends—takes extreme luck and privilege, it just does. And I use the word *privilege* because it's something a lot of people just aren't lucky enough to come by, but we talk about it like everyone gets this. And the truth is, you're more likely to get it if you had a great childhood and loving parents. And separating it from those facts and putting it squarely on the shoulders of worthiness, renders it an indictment of your character.

To admit publicly that you don't really have friends, that you haven't found your people yet, that you've had a lot of the wrong people in your life, is so visceral that I can feel it when

23

I talk about it. I can feel the judgment, the "we don't dare speak of that" formality of the rules we're asked to follow.

There is, of course, no set rulebook, but I know so many of us have gotten similar messages about what friendship means, depending on your culture, your community, and your gender.

The message I saw in media was that friendships took on one of two categories: popular ladies with frenemies, or a group of scrappy weirdos who accepted each other in the ways the world didn't.

As someone who didn't have the foundation of a very tight-knit family, I dreamed of a world where someone would hurt me, minorly, or gravely, and the offender would "have *us* to deal with." I wanted backup. Not just me, alone in the world, realizing that I had to be my own backup.

These thoughts were raging inside of me, all while looking for fictional characters to identify with in popular media and coming up short. *Veronica Mars*, who lost all of her old friends because of trauma, still had her incredible dad and her friend Wallace, whom she saw every day, and they were always by her side, no matter what. Yet, the people around her seemed to imply that this was not enough, this was something unfortunate, a consolation prize, which makes sense, because in high school you can't have just one friend. But it can be hard to watch someone who has so much more than you have being painted as someone who has nothing. So then you have, what? Less than nothing?

What if even the biggest loners you see represented in the world still have their people? Still have people to call if things get bad? Still have someone they see every day, who always chooses them, rallies for them, cheers them up, cheers them on?

And how we define friendship for men and women is radically different. Many media depictions show that friendship for men is watching the game(?), cracking open a cold one(?), no hugs unless they're basically smacking each other on the back in a way that might leave a bruise(?), complaining about how your wife is on your nuts(?), and backing you up in a bar fight. I think I listed them all and god, that's depressing.

Is it any better for women though? Yes, but not by much. The female friendships we often see seem to fall into two categories: 1. Very empowering deep friendships that never have any problems ever, or 2. Friendships that are full of manipulation and competition but also love. In those cases, we have actively woven together toxic behavior with love and said, "Wow that's so wonderfully human! That's love right there." And while I love depictions of how sticky and messy female friendships can be, I don't love that we've been told that it's normal for female friendships to be passive-aggressive competitive sports. Or that we've been shown that "the hot one" has to have "the ugly one" who worships her and keeps her humble. That there is only one hot, cool, kind friend and the other one is an old pile of socks with a few jokes. Good god we have set up a horrific ropes course—to hell with these tropes.

There are of course so many beautiful exceptions in pop culture. Particularly, Anne Shirley and Diana Barry's lifelong, deeply devoted, Platonic Soulmates friendship in *Anne of Green Gables*. (Though, their friendship is arguably two people who are totally in love with each other, and I will forever stand by this correct assumption, but that's for another book.) But if such a Platonic Soulmate exists, where do you find that devotion that sees you through adolescence, into adulthood, into marriages and kids and moving and new careers? Where do you find that magical, poetic friendship where you both grow on parallel tracks—even if they're not the same tracks exactly—into people who still connect deeply, not only as the people you once were, but also as the people you're constantly becoming?

I'm not even the person I was last year or a few months ago, which is true for so many of us who are actively working to unlearn and reprogram things we were told, things we told ourselves, things we allowed ourselves to accept. To have someone who grows with you and changes with you, and you don't lose touch is very rare. It's far more normal, albeit very painful most of the time, to outgrow each other as we grow and heal and change.

We talk about how "we just grew apart" as though it's casual, and while it is in many ways because it's not malicious and it's not abusive, god, is it heartbreaking. That your paths were just not meant to continue to cross. They verged briefly, and that was that. We don't really show that in the media! Oh god, can you imagine?

What if all of the sudden Rachel and Monica from *Friends* just started talking way less, until they didn't talk at all? The TV show would FIX THAT. They would address it like a four-alarm fire had gone off in that impossibly large rent-controlled West Village apartment. It just isn't done (rare exceptions of course exist, such as on *Insecure* and *And Just Like That*, though it's worth noting the latter likely never would've had this plot-line if Kim Cattrall hadn't left the show precisely because a sort-of friendship fallout happened off-camera). And because we rarely see people talk about friendship breakups, we've internalized that it is better to remain in a friendship that isn't working, lest we commit the cardinal sin of ending it.

If faced with a potential friend breakup, many of us will do whatever it takes to mend it, try to fit the square peg into the now very round hole. We've been taught to do anything for the ones we love, even if it's not working anymore. "It takes work," people will say, and they're right. Love, friendships, all of it does. But this is still a dangerous thing to tell people with no further explanation.

Because so many of us, myself included, have internalized that as, "Well, this relationship is killing me, but you know what? I'm gonna make fixing it my full-time job, even though I think relationships are a collaboration between two people making it work, but whatever! I believe this is what love is, so I'm gonna do it!"

We try to make something that is just broken, that maybe we didn't even break, work. Because we've been sold this idea that love is all that matters, so you should give everything you've got to make something work. Even when it's harmful, even when the other person isn't helping with that group project, even when it's possibly just run its course. And we continue to worship at that altar, even though it's covered in broken glass that cuts us every time we kneel.

You don't want to give up too soon either, so you hope that "It'll be worth it, this is just a rough patch." And maybe it is! But a rough patch usually doesn't last for months, causing years of pain.

It can feel like we only have two options: the first being the easy friendship where we've known each other our whole lives and we're always together and it's always great, or the one that isn't quite what we want, but it's the best we have right now, so we have to constantly work on it, even if it's often painful. The first doesn't seem accessible to many of us, or realistic, but the second one seems like a grueling full-time job I want to quit before I even start. What are the benefits? Well, you get to say you have a "best friend." "That's my GIRL right there." You can at least pretend. You can play house. You can bring ice cream over, do face masks, braid each other's hair, and try to make it work, try to make it into what it's supposed to look like.

And I think many of us do that, or have at least tried to. We've tried to be like the friends on TV, the people we wish we were, connected like we think we should be. And we found ourselves, or other people, falling short in the process. Because maybe that doesn't even work for us! Maybe we're not "face masks and ice cream and wearing robes while watching romcoms" kinds of people. Maybe we're not "let's watch the game with a cold one, bro" kinds of people. Maybe we're not built for these archetypes, and then where do we go? How do we navigate this, how do we communicate what we want our ideal friendships to look like if we've never seen them yet? Never experienced them yet? And if you make a new friend as an adult, how do you tell them you haven't really had that yet?

It takes so much vulnerability, in some ways so much more than in a romantic relationship, to say, "Hey, here's what I want our relationship to look like and feel like. Do you want that too?" The anxiety of this concept is so intense. And I felt it firsthand recently.

There's a friend I've made over the last year named Jen. Jen is, ugh, I can't even begin to tell you. She's gorgeous and talented and smart and warm and caring and kind, and we started spending more and more time together. She's always made me feel truly taken care of, truly seen, truly supported.

So, naturally, our friendship made me anxious constantly, but it was absolutely worth it.

One night we were hanging out and I wanted to pick up something I got from a Free Group online (where people in your neighborhood will give away things they don't need anymore as a really beautiful form of mutual aid that I truly love). I wanted to walk the two miles to get there and she said "I'll come with you!" True best friend potential right there. Someone who is so down for whatever because they get to be with you.

While we walked through the city at sunset, seeing the orange sky and the empty streets, walking so fast, in that giddy way where you feel like you have a sidekick, we talked about *Broad City*. I don't remember who brought it up initially, but I said we were both really Abbis, even though I seem like an Ilana.

Jen said she wanted that kind of deep, "seeing you every single day until we both die" best friendship so much, and we hinted, through our referencing of this TV show we both love, that we felt like that with each other. Potentially. Blink and you'd miss it, but I knew what we meant. And I loved the idea of it. And then I immediately went into planning mode.

My mind began to race: *So what should we do now??? Do we get tattoos together? Book a girls trip??? Swap half-heart necklaces?* But just as quickly as I thought that, I worried I was misreading it, worried maybe I wanted that too much, that I was too excited by it.

The more time I spent with Jen the more I just adored her so much and wanted to, I don't know, make it official? But what even is that? The anxiety of what to do, how to do it, what was appropriate, what was acceptable, and would I be rejected if I brought up any of this, or said the wrong thing, caused me to pull away a little bit. I still texted her, but I stopped going to see her as often.

My overthinking had turned into, *Wait, I always initiate our hangs, am I bothering her?* and I started to do it less, and when she didn't pick up that slack, I interpreted it as proof I had been right. But deep down, I knew better. She came to my shows and supported my work online, and any time I asked her advice on my drawings, she wrote back something beautiful, thoughtful, and warm. I would check in with her and ask about her life and get so excited when she would have new art projects out, gush over social media posts of her work, and tell her excessively how talented she was and champion any damn thing she wanted to do.

Finally, I started to realize, "Lane, you have to go see her again. You miss her. She is your friend." So I made plans to go over to her neighborhood for the first time in months and she took me to lunch.

As we talked, she again spoke of wishing for a deep friendship (the kind we both so clearly wanted to have), and I stood there like a thirteen-year-old in platonic love with their best friend, wanting to say, "I mean, I think we have that. Could have that. Do have that." But I didn't. It felt too terrifying, and maybe a little forced to say, "Could I formally apply to be your best friend?"

Because the truth is, after grade school, I don't know how that properly works. Do you just spend more and more time together and it happens and then you just acknowledge that is what happened and you're like *yay!*?

If you entered the workforce in the last twenty or so years, it's likely that you've been working much more than the typical forty hours your parents and their parents were expected to

work in order to "make it." And somehow within that sometimes sixty- to eighty-hour work week, you're still expected
to have rich friendships and lives, but how can you do that
when everyone is tired and busy? Each week we might only
have so many spare hours, only have so much energy that it
can feel daunting to devote it to a new person who we hope
will become someone meaningful to us, but we can't be sure.
"Life gets in the way" is seemingly truer all the time. And "just
hanging out and seeing what happens" becomes less and less
possible, since every friendship you set out to develop takes
time, planning, and effort, so you rightfully might be hesitant
to take a new one on.

As Jen walked me to the subway, I asked if she wanted to
do something again soon. I'd often texted her some places that
looked cool in the city—art installations, museum exhibits,
best friend things. I wanted to see the world with her, alongside her, maybe, if she wanted to also. She said she'd love to, as
soon as she finished up a project.

And again, the anxiety surfaced. What if she didn't mean
it, and work being hectic was a very polite way of saying no?
But more than that, what if I cared more than she did? This
comes up so often in friendships, where your schedules just
can't connect, and it genuinely may be that they want to see
you more, but it's just not the right timing yet. Like with
dating, if you're meant to be close friends, they'll make time
and you'll make time, the scheduling will be easy, or at least
become easier. If it's meant to be, it'll happen.

There is so much about forming friendships that is akin
to romantic relationships, even though we love to separate
them, as though friendship is easy and innate, and romantic
relationships are complex and daunting. But trying to get the

You Will Find Your People

courage to slide someone a sheet of paper that says, "Do you want to be my friend? Check yes or no" across the table is no less terrifying than asking a romantic partner, "What are we? Because I would like to be together." It requires the same risk, the same courage, the same hopefulness that it will work out and we will be accepted.

There's no cheat code for it, or I would've found one, trust me. We just have to jump and hope they catch us.

As of writing this, Jen and I are still friends. I support her fiercely through the energy I emit when I stare lovingly at her posts. I wish it was as seamless of a friends-to-best-friends pipeline as it is in the movies, but maybe right now it's exactly what it needs to be. Maybe we didn't get to meet each other when we were thirteen, maybe we're both nervous or only I am, or maybe this is just how our friendship begins. And it takes years to develop, twists and turns leading us to become even closer years from now when the timing is right.

And maybe we get to write our story together exactly as the people we are. And maybe it's a really, really good one. And if not, we have to trust we'll get another shot to be brave again with someone else.

32

On Keeping People at a Distance So You Don't Get Hurt Again

I want your warm, but it will only make me colder when it's over. —Fiona Apple, "Love Ridden"

When I was a kid around age nine or so, I remember that pen pals were very much a normal thing that wasn't loser-y. Except now that I think about it, maybe it kind of was? I highly doubt the Hot Girls (subjective) in my high school were emailing with some mountain girl from Montana and dreaming about what her life must be like and if she was like Kirsten from the American Girl dolls, but with more electricity and indoor plumbing. If you were somewhat romantic, somewhat uncool, somewhat queer, or just a very curious sort of person, pen pals were marketed directly to you, like a targeted ad. (But sent to you by your Girl Scouts troop leader or something? I honestly don't remember how it happened, but one day I just started getting the addresses of young girls who wanted to write to strangers. In retrospect, I bet this whole operation could've done with some more screening.)

We were told it was educational to speak with someone our own age who had a slightly different or very different life than we did. Often the letters were handwritten, with stickers, photos, and little snapshots—lovingly prepared scrapbooks that peered into the parts of our life we were comfortable sharing with an absolute stranger.

I never felt like my pen pal letters were that good. I've always had messy handwriting, which I attribute to my hands being unable to catch up with the speed with which my brain processes things, so it just comes out as, "Here's two legible letters and a bunch of frustrated scribbles because I tried and then tapped out." But my pen pals (I must've had at least three at different points in time) always went all out, with the aforementioned stickers, delicate little doodles, and great penmanship—and even when it wasn't super legible, it was so dreamy to see another girl's handwriting, to feel chosen. Being somebody's someone, even if I knew it didn't necessarily mean as much to them, felt incredible. You'd discuss your town, how many relatives you had, books you liked, and that was that. It was very clean, very formal, and for better or worse it was finite.

I've heard stories of pen pals who kept it up for years, which sounds beautiful, but my experiences with pen pals were fleeting. I'd get glimpses into their worlds, and one day, whether intentional or not, my pen pal would just stop writing. Or they died? You just didn't know. But you couldn't text them or email them. (Well, you could, but 1. You didn't have their email and 2. That would ruin the mystique of what you were doing and 3. Could possibly be creepy, because they stopped writing, as was their right.) Pen pals just not writing back truly was the original ghosting, and it cut like a very cute but sharp knife.

Something about this potential for intimacy combined with the safety of distance stuck with me as I navigated the disappointments of my childhood and teenage years. And any time I moved, I often found myself becoming very good friends with people *after* I'd left, even if I was only sort of friends with them when I lived in close proximity. I'm sure on some level I felt like this was the best of both worlds: the belonging and companionship and inside jokes and a place to put my thoughts and feelings, without the danger of getting too close and being disappointed by them, or worse.

I'd seen enough of that. So I was ~Going Online~.

I had always loved parasocial relationships, long before I knew that's what they were. Parasocial relationships are relationships with people you don't really know but feel like you know. These are most often relationships with celebrities whose work you love, but I'd argue they can just as easily be people you interact with on social media, support groups, any kind of online community you have at your fingertips, but it usually doesn't go much further than that. You might not know their full name or even where they live or what they look like, but you really like talking to them here and there, or reading the things they write. And these friendships can be meaningful, even if they don't meet the classic definition.

The beauty of relationships like this is that at any moment you can post something in these groups or pages and have an instant community, instant feedback, instant support. But because you don't have the "we talk every day" or the "we see each other every Friday night for wings and manicures" (this sounds like a very messy day and I do not know why that's where my brain went, but here we are) connection, it can be easy to forget they exist and easy to still feel very alone.

Online-only friendships feel more tenuous to me because by all accounts, they are. Someone who doesn't really know you will only know you by what you post, by what they read, and how they read it on that particular day. So the potential for them to take something you said the wrong way and decide they don't like you anymore is very real. Those things happen. And if you struggle with the fear in your real-world friendships that one day you'll say something and someone will misconstrue it and you'll be punished, seeing that fear realized online is just as heartbreaking. Even if you don't fully know the person. Because it will activate the part of you that thinks it's normal for things to be that tenuous, and that fear can exacerbate those feelings in your real-world friendships once you find them.

Because yes, it is possible to have abandonment issues with total strangers. I know it well.

That said, if you have such friendships and you're able to put those fears aside and weather those storms if and when they arise, it's very easy to want to take things to the next level. And that could look different for all of us: Maybe it's actually talking on the phone or texting instead of commenting on each other's posts, just something that feels a little more like "the real thing," even if it's long-distance.

My first long-distance friendship was with Delia. And it's worth noting we met through a man when I was a teenager, and I think there's a reason for that.

Women are very often geared toward the idea that you should pour everything you have into men: Get their attention; keep it; be surrounded by male friends. Because men are "less complicated" and men thinking you're cool is the greatest currency you could have! "Women can't be trusted, they're so dramatic, too catty, it's always something with them, they're two-faced and men just tell you if they have a problem with you." These internalized beliefs coupled with my deeply flawed belief that romantic love would save me, far more than friendship ever would or could, caused me to spend my teens and early twenties pursuing dating websites and social media as a way to meet male "friends"—in retrospect, this meant men who would get all the benefits of having me as their girlfriend, but without any dates or need to physically show up or provide any further investment. They got the emotional intimacy, the emotional labor, the hot girl who listened and entertained them, all the things men get from women they keep at a distance, while they did nothing in return except exist. And we allow this because we hope one day it turns into more, that this is perhaps the beginning of our love story.

For all I know, it suited these male "friends" in the same way it did me: getting to have a relationship without the scary parts. One night during this time, while talking on the phone with one such male "friend," Kevin, who I'd seen exactly one very flattering photo of online and developed a deep immediate intimacy with (zero stars, do not recommend), he said, "Hey, my friend Dex is here, and you actually remind me a lot of her. I think you guys would like each other a lot, should I put her on?" And I said, "Sure," without hesitation, and I guess she did, too, because the next thing I knew she was on the line.

Her name, I would find out later in the phone call, is actually Delia. So I was confused when I heard him call her Dex when introducing her to me. Immediately my brain registered this as, "Oh wow, he knows her so well they have nicknames for each other. Her name is Delia and he called her *DEX*? AND they're in the same room together hanging out? What a very close friendship they clearly have, and I am obviously on the outside of what is a deeply established bond. They must hold all the secrets to True Friendship, and I am simply auditioning for a minor role."

Delia would tell me years later that the only people who called her Dex at that time had known her in middle school, and one day Kevin overheard one of her very few middle school friends call her Dex and decided to use that very intimate nickname, which she felt was bizarre—a sort of forced intimacy on his part she never really understood and chose to let go. But back then, it felt like everyone but me was doing life "right," so to hear years later that actually their friendship was full of weird frustrations, false indicators of intimacy where there were actually none, and the "eh, this will work for now" elements—all of which were actually much more relatable than I could have known when we met—was a revelation.

As I remember, my connection with Delia was instantaneous. We bonded over nineties movies, Nina Simone and Amy Sedaris, and wearing a thick coat of armor over a lifetime of trauma and isolation that left us both simultaneously open to anything and scared of everything. What was the worst that could happen from talking to a cool girl who lives far away for a few minutes? She'd disappoint me? Happened before. It was worth it to roll the dice because what if this time was different?

A few minutes turned into a few hours, walking around my apartment, sharing everything the way you do when something about the connection feels special, feels different, feels destined. I can only assume Kevin stood next to Delia most of that night, eyes glazed over, having now been iced out of being the very special boy or whatever and realizing that his role had been relegated to being a means to an end. He had absolutely wanted this phone call to be a testimonial: "See? You should date me, I know cool women. I'm a good guy," which Delia now recalls he had her do with a few women at that time. And instead, we were both like, "I'm good," the way you respond when someone tries to hand you a flyer on the subway.

I don't even remember the end of our call. To me, we spoke once and just never stopped. Our entire friendship has just been one really long phone call I wanted to last forever. But I do know we exchanged numbers, and I know she told me, warned me even, in a nonchalant, no-big-deal way that I probably wouldn't know her for very long, because she doesn't trust anyone, and people are always assholes. I remember smiling and saying, "OK, let's see."

The thing is, when most people hear you say things like that, I'm sure they run. I'm sure they get upset: "How dare you assume that of me? That hurts my feelings." And I bet it does. When you don't know what it's like to have to warn people to be more careful with you, because you've been hurt so badly before but you really would love them to be different, to be better, you hear that and you want to run. But I knew what it was like to have to say that, how many times she'd probably said it, hoping someone saw past it and proved her wrong. I heard her say that, and I wanted to stay.

Delia and I would watch movies together on the phone (ten stars, recommend), I would read her writing and I'd swoon, and she'd read mine and she loved it. I'd never really shown my writing to anyone, so it felt like what I imagined Fran Lebowitz being friends with Toni Morrison was like. Someone this talented and wise and incredible thinks I'm a great writer? Heaven.

When we first met, Delia had these magical friends, Margaret and Zoe, and I can describe them to you as though they were characters in a movie I watched over and over again, because I was vicariously living through what I perceived as Delia having normal friends and normal experiences I didn't fully relate to yet. Margaret was an artist who had red hair and was very cool and had a job doing something with pets, maybe? Photography? I guess that part of the movie wasn't as interesting to me as her haircut, which I remember being very cool. And Zoe was a Cool Girl, as I aspired to be on the rare occasion I left my house. But she *actually* left her house and went to parties and gallery openings; she did her makeup every single day, always put together incredible outfits, and was seemingly never too sad to put on eyeliner, etc.

I'd listen to Delia talk about Zoe's cool New York City job working at a fashion magazine and Margaret doing . . . again I have no idea, and it was like my own private *Sex and the City*. Now, was I twelve years old and incapable of actually going to bars and having friends and a cool NYC job, so I had to watch them do it on budget HBO? No, I was just out of high school, fully able to do those things but deeply healing from some traumas and feeling like my life was on pause, while others got to keep living theirs. It was like watching another version of me who wasn't a girl, interrupted.

For years, our friendship ebbed and flowed through great times and worse times, and we were never in the same room and rarely even on the same coast. And in that time, Delia became extremely depressed, and her "people always disappoint, people don't stick around" beliefs became even more founded. As her depression grew, Margaret and Zoe no longer saw her as "fun," so they left her behind. By that time, Delia just had me and a few other long-distance friends to lean on. Both of us were definitely not in the majority of what was normal at all. This was not the crew of girls you'd see every weekend over margaritas. I had no idea what that type of friendship was like, or when/if it was coming, with her or anyone else.

This was an extension of a habit I had formed with my pen pals: A lot of my most intimate friendships were with people who lived far away. I can totally see now that subconsciously the distance made them feel less threatening to me. If I didn't get too close to them, and better yet, physically could not get close to them, I had much better odds of them not hurting me—safety at all costs.

Since we first spoke, Delia and I have been in the same room three times over the course of many years, and she's still pretty much the closest thing I've got to "we've known each other since we were kids." It's funny what "kids" means to people at different ages in their lives. I'll watch a kids movie now and see the thirteen-year-old girl say, "I'm practically an adult now!" and I'll be both frightened (side note: if you are a teenage girl please don't let some twenty-four-year-old man tell you that you are an adult) and amused because I know I was a child until I was twenty-one at least, and maybe even until twenty-five, which is when your brain is fully formed.

Distance or not, traditional or not, having the baseline safety of someone, somewhere out there, who even briefly satisfied that need to be seen, to be supported, made it much easier for us to talk on the phone about our day and really jump ahead to the type of intimacy you have when you're five years in.

Delia is now my oldest friend. But was it that simple? Did I cross "I made a friend" off a list and move on? Not at all. The friendship ebbed and flowed, and sometimes we wouldn't talk for years. We often talk about "my oldest friend" in terms of years—"We've known each other since we were twelve!"—and the expectation is you knew each other that whole time, that you saw each other through it all. But sometimes that's not as easy to maintain, especially with distance, though you wish it were.

We'd talk, and then stop talking for a while, or she'd push me away, and in that space between, we still hoped for reconnection. In the meantime, I would start reconnecting with friends from my past who already kind of knew me and who I remembered being pretty cool, maybe? The bar was beneath the earth's core at the time, so I just needed bodies to fill the space, like a club owner bringing in people from the street to fill his floundering DJ night. Until I met Seth.

Seth and I met when we were doing improv together, so I was naturally suspicious. One night, while we were working the box office for no pay in exchange for classes, Seth told me he thought I was an incredible comedian and everyone else there was an asshole. I assumed it was a line and he was just another guy who didn't see me as a peer, but as someone who was dying to sleep with him if he gave me the slightest compliment. He told me he was forming his own improv team and he wanted me on it. Again, suspicious. After asking around and finding out the coach was a woman I really liked and the team had some really cool people, I joined. Thank goodness I did. Seth became one of my favorite people to do scenes with. He was silly and fun and truly respected me. I quickly realized he wasn't hitting on me before, he was treating me the way most men probably treat other men: "Hey, you're awesome. Let's work together." Just basic respect and adoration. No strings.

Since he was wonderful and there were so many good things about him, you won't be surprised to know that we only became friends after I moved away. That time in my life was so full of horrible people and just the worst luck, it was nearly impossible for me to trust anyone. I kept worrying, *What if I'm making the wrong decisions again?* But sometimes life allows you to form the kinds of connections that are just close enough to what you want, while also being exactly what you currently need. Seth and I reconnected on a more personal level when I told him I was moving and he said, "Aw man, that sucks! I always really liked working with you. Do you have a ride to the airport yet?" When I told him I didn't, he scoffed, "No one has offered you a ride to the airport? These fuckin' people. I'm taking you to the airport."

Seth picked me up as he said he would and got us snacks and drove me to the airport. Such a simple thing was light-years beyond anything I'd experienced before and created a bond that I continued via texts and phone calls once I got to NYC. Seth was a very curious sort of person (me too, respect) who didn't really have friends. He talked to me and maybe one other person on a regular basis, and when I asked him if he ever got lonely, he replied, "No. Because I had a great family." And the difference between us hit me like a ton of bricks.

Look, I'm sure there are people reading this who had that great family and still need friends, of course. But it was a huge moment for me, not necessarily because that was why I needed friends, but it was surely why I needed them so badly. So badly that I'd routinely settle for scraps and crumbs, neglect and abuse, whatever, as long as you'll allow me to sit with you, thank you so much! And after hearing Seth say that, knowing that he got it, I, in the smallest possible way, began to forgive myself for being so "needy," aka someone who needed something we literally all need: community.

That said, I can't explain to you why Seth and I still never felt like close friends in my mind, except to say it boiled down to a few things:

1. He lived so far away, and while I'd unknowingly needed that distance for many reasons, it was a catch-22 because those friendships can largely feel like you hallucinated this person in a time of crisis, the way Tom Hanks started to befriend a volleyball in that movie I did not see.
2. Seth had a wealth of empathy and kindness and support but came from such a safe, loving, consistent background and I didn't, so I never felt fully seen in that way, which kept me from getting any closer than we were.

I have often struggled with being able to fully connect to people who haven't been through anything close to what I've been through, which, to be fair, always seemed like very few people (of course, I know from writing *How to Be Alone* that it's not *so* few; there are so many of us, we just rarely meet for whatever reason. I personally assume the reason is we're all pretty terrified of human beings). And not because surviving trauma makes you better or worse, but because trauma can make you feel like you're weird, unlike anyone else, and no one could possibly relate to you or see you and give you what you need.

If someone says, "Ugh my dad's being the worst right now" and you know it's because their dad is just being a little overprotective from a place of love while your version of "being the worst" involves near-death experiences, how the hell can you get close to that person? And often people do not really consider these potential differences before they speak. In a new friendship it can be so important to know what someone else has experienced before you assume that your experience is monolithic. If I had a friend whose dad was dying of cancer, I don't think it would be too much trouble to not complain about how my very healthy dad was calling me too much to tell me he loves me and it was annoying me? I think that's a pretty easy lift. And having to explain all of those nuances to a friend who's already in your life and risking rejection or them not understanding that, or them calling you dramatic or some other shade of "Ugh why can't you just be like me and be very lucky?" is often not worth the energy expended.

To Seth's credit, though, he never did that. He has the most empathy I've ever encountered from someone who had, by their own admission, "A great family and a wonderful childhood." In my experience, it seems that empathy is often derived from lived experience, and many times is born from not having empathy given to you in similar circumstances. Empathy is the currency of people who've been there, and wish things had gone differently. And yet many times, there are people who've been to hell and back and have somehow returned with very little empathy for others who struggle in that way or, in Seth's case, they have actively developed it because they cared enough to do so.

Most people I've met have some baseline empathy, so there is a spectrum. Many people's empathy baseline is based primarily on their own personal experiences, because that's where empathy originates. "I've been through this, so I know how it feels." To cultivate further empathy, broader empathy, requires opening your eyes to *other* peoples' experiences. People who've had their eyes opened to the unfairness or "bad" in the world, often do not think of empathy as something that's optional. It is innate, required. So if you haven't, it is very much a choice to say, "this has been my experience in the world, but it is not the only experience and I am interested in seeing the world outside myself, doing the work, increasing my own awareness, and then reading and learning about things that might make me uncomfortable. Because it is even more uncomfortable to live them."

People who opt out of doing this further work may still be empathetic to things they've experienced, their own socio-economic class, religion, race, etc. But true empathy is larger than your own experience. So if you're willing to turn a blind eye, it might not be because you don't empathize with anyone, it could be that you don't want to broaden your experience to encompass anyone else's pain. When you love someone, expanding that empathy for your loved one who may be going through something you don't understand, should come with the territory. But many times, it does not.

It can be so hard to try and develop a sense of community if we can't acknowledge how much we're impacted by the ways each of us is able to walk through the world. And if we're going to be friends with someone who walks through the world with greater ease, it is imperative they bring with them greater empathy for us as well.

When I asked Seth how it was possible that he had so much empathy for situations he had no experience with, he told me it was because he chose to actively cultivate it, it was a choice he made to care enough to have it, and it blew me away. It echoed every sense I'd had that he was extraordinary.

Though he was far away, I clung to moments every few years when Seth would come to visit NYC and we would play like excited little kids. I always know I feel good about someone when my little kid self can come hang out, and by that I mean, when I'm free to be goofy and unfiltered and not worry if I'm accidentally doing something wrong, or if I'm being judged.

Finding someone with whom you can just drop all that—the overwhelming exhaustion of trying to be fine and perfect and normal, as defined by very antiquated standards—was extremely liberating. And when my social battery would run out and so would his, we would say *OK, bye* and part ways and it was totally fine, no one was mad. A dream.

Each time Seth came to visit, he'd say maybe one day he would move here and we could hang out all the time, and I loved that idea but knew it probably wouldn't happen. And even if it did, would it be as great as when he visited? Would I be able to show up in person for this friendship regularly if we lived close by? Would he? And each time he would head back home, I was once again ejected from this elevated place where I was loved and seen and safe and able to fully be myself, back into a world where I never really felt that with anyone, and had no idea how to find more people in my city who might fit that bill.

NYC was once again me versus the world, instead of us versus the world. And while I knew our friendship didn't actually disappear when he flew back, the fact that he lived very far away somehow made it feel like it did. I lacked the object permanence to be able to know that just because something disappeared from view doesn't mean it stopped existing in the world.

And here's the thing: In the big picture, long-distance friends absolutely do count. They do. And we don't see that reflected enough in the world, so it's important for me to say to you they absolutely count. It is equally important, however, to say that it is also completely valid to sometimes feel like it's still not enough, or feel like it "doesn't count." Not because it's nothing, because it's so, so much. Long-distance friends may be so much more than you've had before, while also still not being nearly enough for the kind of friendship you've always wanted.

It is completely possible to love your long-distance friendship and still wish it was a local friendship. To wish those people lived closer, not as a passing thing you text each other sometimes—*"Aww, I wish I was there"*—but in a deep, very real way, and it's hard not to wonder why you don't get to have it all.

I still regard Delia and Seth and many of my other long-distance friends as some of my most intimate, my most kindred. Perhaps in part because the only way we've lasted this long is our ability to nurture the friendship even in distance, even after long periods of time when we don't talk as much. We're always able to pick the ball back up where we left off.

I know Delia and Seth are out there, rooting for me, even if we've only been in the same room together a few short times. Even if our friendship is often them sending me jokes and cool photos from the sixties, or telling me they're coming to NYC and they're going to come by my show while they're in town to see me. I know that these are deep, wonderful connections that I hold extremely dear, and it is absolutely OK if you hold long-distance friends in the same very high regard.

And it is also absolutely OK to say to yourself, "These long-distance friendships are beautiful, they are, AND I also still want a friend who lives close by, a friend who drops by with soup, a friend who can come with me to the hospital, a friend to go to the movies with last minute. These normal things, I deserve to have them. I do not have to settle *only* for friendships that are not fully what I need, fully what I want."

It's wonderful to be able to share some parts of your life with someone in any way, but in a long-distance friendship you're often just getting the pieces of their life. You can joke and watch movies and analyze each other's lives, but you miss out on the shared experiences of doing that over dinner, or coffee, or staying out 'til three A.M. and so much happened that you were both there for. You miss out on those memories you make in person, where it wasn't just a story you gave them the highlight reel of later.

And then comes the challenging part: finding the courage to cultivate in-person, local friendships. Someone who hugs you when you need it, and not just through the phone. Someone who can be in the same room with you, and you get to see their facial cues and nonverbal cues, and they get to see yours. Being able to be all the messy parts of yourself that you usually can hide with distance, in the same room, fully loved and held this time.

To know that this is possible. And allow it to be so.

For me, it was so important to finally realize why I was exclusively forming connections with people who were physically, and oftentimes emotionally, at a distance as an insurance plan designed to keep me safe. Putting up those walls keep out the bad, yes, but they can also keep out the good. So if you've noticed you tend to pick the equivalent of "you wouldn't know her, she lives in another state" friendships, reflect on why you are choosing them. Maybe it's just because no one in your area is like you, or you don't have access to finding people who are.

That's extremely true for many of us. But if it's not just that, ask those deeper questions of yourself.

Do you feel people wouldn't like you if they really knew you, or vice versa? Do you feel like you don't deserve to have friendships the way other people have them? Do these distant friendships check a box for you, so that you can tell people you have friends, and avoid dealing with any intimacy issues you might have? It's completely valid and understandable if any of these resonate, and you're definitely not alone. But it's only once you examine these patterns that you're able to address the root causes of these choices. If it's any of the above, then affirming your worthiness is your mission.

You deserve to have everything you want, even if it feels scary, even if you've been hurt. And especially because it feels so scary, especially because you've been hurt. I'm rooting for you most of all.

Yes, Animals Can
Be Your (Best) Friends

You are my favorite person, you are my best friend and
I love you, and you are perfect and I love you.
  —Me to my dog all the time, as often as possible

When I first got my dog, Lights, she was a foster-fail, which
is a term for a dog who you agree to foster for a little while
until they find their forever home, only to quickly realize you
are their forever home. This is such a perfect comparison for
when we become casual friends with someone and don't think
too much about it, and then much to our delight, they become
the lifelong friends we weren't expecting.

When I found Lights, I had a complicated mixture of people in my life who were "potentially my friends I think?" and
"friends, but I'm frustrated with them" and "very good friends
but I'm still unsure how to utilize them if I need something
or I'm going through something hard." I had no idea this little dog would become a beautiful bridge to the type of deep,
meaningful, reliable connection I'd wanted so badly but wasn't
sure how to get.

In the years since getting a dog, I've heard other people say
that they were similarly afraid of, or had a hard time connecting

with people, and they too found with animals the wonderful companionship that had often eluded them with humans.

There are lower stakes with animals. They're innately loving, and the potential for them to suddenly leave you because they met someone who they think is cooler than you is slim, due to the fact that they live with you.

Adopting this deeply loving, affectionate dog who wasn't afraid to show how much she cared about me, and truly appreciated everything I did for her, was my first experience with consistency, my first experience with reciprocity. Every day I assumed I would come home and she would be in a mood, or suddenly hate me, or want to go hang out with someone else, because my abandonment issues were formidable. But every day she was so excited to see me, every day she loved me just the same, if not even more.

When I accidentally stepped on her tiny foot, and apologized a million times, I assumed she would hate me or hold it over me for months—now I would surely be punished. But she never did. An apology was enough because she knew me and she knew I didn't mean to hurt her, because of how I'd always treated her before. Because I had shown her consistency. She still loved me, and we both moved on. Well, she moved on. I still felt bad for weeks, but you get it.

Every time I gave her dog massages, or pets, or cuddles, or comforted her when she felt bad, it was reciprocated and appreciated so deeply. When I was sick, just as I'd cared for her, she would run to cuddle with me to heal me as fast as she could. There was no resentment or score keeping, but there was an understanding that she had my back, and I had hers, always. If I had it to give, she'd get it. And if she had it to give, I'd get it. I can't tell you how revolutionary that felt to me.

And it made me realize that yes, there can be friends who just keep loving you, who are steady and consistent, even if you don't have energy for them all the time, or you don't see them as often as you'd like. When you come back they will still be there. There can be friends who will see you mess up and accept a genuine apology and a promise to do better because they know you and they know your heart, and people make mistakes. There can be friends who show up for you just as much as you show up for them. And it feels so much better than not knowing where you stand, or worrying what small misstep might break this delicate thing.

Even now, I'll have moments when Lights really loves one of my friends a lot and I'll wonder if one day she'll love them more than me and leave me and I'll be alone. Similarly, those fears might still be there years into a friendship, but having a dog has taught me to weather those feelings and see them as just that: my feelings. They are mine to deal with, mine to observe, and watch them pass by. They aren't necessarily based on facts, or even based on who I am in the present. They might just be, and usually are, remnants of past hurts that come up every now and again, unhealed parts of me asking to be soothed. And I soothe them by reminding myself of what is real. And what is real is that those feelings always pass, and this is truly just a tiny animal who wants me to love her, and who wants to love me back.

And if that exists in a dog, then it must exist in people too. And you deserve to find them as much as they deserve to find you.

Friends Who Are
Good on Paper

I hang around for another round, until something stops
me. —The Cardigans, "Hanging Around"

When *How to Be Alone* came out, I started making friends
with people who had read it and found me because of it. They
were in the unique position of having read about where I'd
come from, what I needed and wanted in a friendship, and
had presumably had the conversation with themselves about
whether they had it to give me, and decided yes, they did, and
yes, they would. The same way that if I finally met Fiona Apple,
I'd be extra nice to her because I know she's been through a
lot and doesn't feel comfortable around most people. And yes,
I've thought about how I would be Fiona Apple's friend many
times, I think that's clear.

It seemed like the dream: to be able to hand people a guide
to your past hurts, your needs, and your want for connections,
so you don't have to go through it every time, like a friendship
intake. I thought it would be like skipping a million steps with
someone. They'd already read the "job requirements" and they
were applying, knowing they'd be great at it. But somehow,

that forethought is not always what happened, and I was again left questioning why.

Years later, I would read that Fiona Apple had the same hope when she released her first album. She thought everyone would finally understand her, and people would want to be her friend, but it didn't exactly turn out that way. And I realized what she might have meant by this when I became friends with Rosemary.

Rosemary and I met because we had mutual friends and she said she really related to my first book, which seemed like a good enough foundation to me. I liked her for so many reasons. She was fearless and eternally confident. She knew she was entitled to whatever she wanted in life and didn't hesitate for a second to ask for it, which, as someone who struggles with both, was intoxicating to watch. And the more we hung out, the more I felt like "Wow, this is what it feels like to walk through the world feeling free and safe and like you can do and have anything? This feels amazing!"

It took me a long while to realize a lot of that came so easily to Rosemary because her parents were insanely rich. Like a lot of very wealthy people, she never mentioned it, so I was thinking we were both just two artists trying to make it in the big city. I assumed she was fearless and didn't care what anyone else thought or felt, because she was brave, and I was constantly afraid and worried about other people's feelings because I wasn't brave. The level of incorrect thinking here would prove to haunt me.

I've seen this so many times in my past friendships, where on paper there's so much about this friendship that is exciting and checks a lot of boxes, but something about it never feels quite right and I'm not sure why: the Good-On-Paper friend.

If you've never had a good-on-paper friend or don't know what one is, first of all congratulations! Second of all, I bet you have and just didn't know it. Here are some telltale signs they're a good-on-paper friend:

1. **You have enough in common that you should get along great, but you don't really.** Maybe you have mutual friends, or work in similar fields, but something about it never quite feels right.

2. **You misunderstand each other a lot.** Many times, being "good on paper" is really about thinking you're on the same wavelength, but something about your dynamic keeps you bumping up against each other and you don't understand why.

3. **They're the type of person you'd want to be friends with.** It's like seeing something at a thrift store that you love on the hanger but not on you. It's a beautiful piece but it doesn't feel good when you put it on. And you want to be the person who feels good in it. But you're just not.

4. **The ways you give and receive love don't match up.** We put so much emphasis on liking someone, but just because you like someone doesn't mean they can give what you need to feel loved, and vice versa. Maybe someone's number one thing they need to feel loved is consistency but unfortunately you have a hard time doing what you say you'll do, even when you love someone. So you can both care for each other, but what you need and what they can give doesn't match up.

5. **You're not sure if you're friends or if you kind of hate them.** Are their jokes playful or are they kind of a horrible person? Or are they kind of a horrible person in a fun way I can live with? I guess time will tell!

6. **You've known them a long time.** Just because you've known someone forever doesn't mean what you have is good, no more than having something in your fridge forever makes it good. Check the expiration date.

7. **You feel like their sidekick, not an equal.** Some people want to be the sidekick in theory, but if it's starting to feel less like you're a team and more like you're the side character in someone else's story, that could be a good sign this isn't working.

8. **They're nice to you but mean to everyone else.** If you've experienced this one, you know. And I wish I didn't know, but I do.

So why do we tolerate a good-on-paper friend? Often, because they're better than nothing and we think we can work with it, like an ugly couch we found on the side of the road that we tell ourselves we can upcycle into something cool, like an HGTV host. There's this feeling many of us know very well: the feeling that you should finally "settle" on one romantic partner to be with, even if just for a while, so you can finally say you're not single anymore, and other people won't ask you any further questions. They'll just be happy they don't have to "worry about you anymore," because you found someone, anyone, box checked. This can absolutely happen with your friendships as well.

Rosemary was a perfect example of a good-on-paper friend. In theory, Rosemary was the type of friend I'd dreamed of: someone who saw me, supported me, and wanted to be my friend. But sometimes the good-on-paper friend is someone who wants to be your friend so much, but they aren't able to be the kind of friend you need. And so you can either cling to their good intentions or acknowledge that current proof is worth far more than future potential. But it can take a while to spot that, and it's easy to get caught up in anything that might be a sign that there's real friendship potential and you just need time to grow together.

Rosemary and I became closer and closer as time went on, so when I found out that I needed to get surgery due to a recent traumatic event and I was very scared, she seemed like a person I could reach out to. When I finally got up the courage to tell her how scared I was, she said, "Lane, I would love to come with you to the hospital for your surgery, because years ago when I was in the hospital, no one came to be with me and I wanted that so badly." I cried, thinking she understood, she got it, and finally here was someone who said they wanted to help and would actually do it. After meeting people in the past who'd said they wanted to help, only to take and take and take, this time seemed like someone who wanted to take every opportunity to do for someone else what they wish someone had done for them. That sounded like the way I thought, the way I did things, and even though we were different in so many ways, I assumed our motivations, our worldviews, were similar. Good on paper.

In the days before the surgery, Rosemary was so excited to help. She told me she would bring me a ton of my favorite snacks and asked what they were. I was allowed to receive care. And it was finally starting now. She was going to come to my house and we would go to the hospital together from there.

And then she showed up that morning and said, oops, she'd forgotten the snacks.

I thought, *Oh that's fine! You're HERE! For my surgery. Goodness, bless you, you saint! Who on earth would even do that???* She sat with me in the hospital and had brought me a stuffed animal we named Tim Curry Tiger, and I don't remember why, except that it was a tiger and it was funny to pretend Tim Curry had embodied him, and to do our respective Tim Curry impressions.

When it was time for surgery, Rosemary went to the waiting room. And for a moment, I felt semi-normal. This is what friendship was supposed to be. I shouldn't be this nervous or this panicked that I was taking more than my fair share of friendship, or wondering what I had to do to "make it up to her," I reassured myself. This kind of "Am I doing things correctly?" anxiety was so common for me and is common for anyone who hasn't had many healthy connections just yet. The fear that the problem is you and your lack of experience with love and friendship.

After some additional traumatic things at the hospital that we will not go into (but just know it was not a chill day), they released me and we were able to head home. Twenty minutes after we got in the car, I was suddenly very aware that I had to pee very badly, but I didn't want to stop the car. I just wanted to be home, and we'd be home in an hour or so, and trying to find a public bathroom in Manhattan with the crutches I now absolutely required to function wasn't my idea of a great time.

Several minutes later, Rosemary said to me, frustrated, "Are we going to be home soon? I have emails I need to send, and this is taking a long time." I immediately launched into, "Oh my goodness, I hope so, yeah I'm sure, yes." And told myself to not stop to go to the bathroom, I needed to just hurry up and get home so my friend could work! ("See? I'm doing it wrong!" echoed through my recently surgery-d body.)

I was told months later by a nurse friend of mine that a big part of my surgery, and maybe all surgery, is that they are required to have you go to the bathroom after surgery. Something about the anesthesia will cause a delayed reaction in realizing you have to pee and may even result in not being able to pee. You're not supposed to leave the hospital until you're able to, but I did not know that, and they just told me to go. So, that was cute and professional!

Not knowing any of this, I finally had to ask the car to stop, and Rosemary angrily sighed, like I was being annoying. I struggled to get out of the SUV by myself, on crutches, and hobbled into a restaurant to use their bathroom. Thankfully, they let me use it, but once I got in there and navigated getting my clothes off in crutches and a cast, I couldn't pee, and I sobbed like I had failed. Because at the time, I didn't know what was happening was normal and not my fault. I hurried back into the car, knowing I'd disappointed Rosemary with my human body and my very long surgery.

When we finally got home, Rosemary raced ahead of me, not to hold the door or anything, but instead asking, "Where's your office so I can send these emails for work?" I raced, on crutches, to show her, while she left me alone in the living room to fend for myself. For hours.

If I needed water, or a snack, or my medication, or to go to the bathroom, I had to get up and get it. Rosemary was working and could not be bothered. When she left, I thanked her two thousand times for being there for me, but something was wrong, and I knew it.

In the days that followed, I wasn't taking my pain meds and frequently collapsed on the floor from extreme pain. I'd always struggled with feeling like my pain wasn't real. I can handle anything, survive anything, so Rosemary acting like my pain was negligible and OK to ignore reinforced in my mind that I must not need the medication at all. Several times, my next-door neighbor found me and helped me get up. I retreated even more after that, unable to fully process how painful that surgery day was for me.

I buried the suspicion that Rosemary hadn't behaved very well that day, could've maybe done things a bit differently, slightly better, as deep down as I could manage. She was my friend and she was there for me, even if it wasn't perfect. That was friendship, sure.

A few days after the surgery, my friend Audrey offered to come by to help as soon as she found out I'd had an operation. I'd stopped telling people what I was going through, internalizing that it was no big deal. Audrey did not think it was "no big deal" at all.

Audrey was a neighbor of mine in my previous apartment and was always lovely and kind and warm, but I didn't know her very well, at least not yet, so I didn't know what to expect. I thought I knew Rosemary much better because we'd spent so much more time together. She was the one who promised to come through, made a show of coming through, told me what I was getting, and then didn't provide it. Audrey simply said she'd come over and be there. And I cautiously accepted.

Audrey brought me a ton of food and slept over on the couch, so if I needed anything, she'd be there. My dog loves her so much she slept with Audrey on the couch all night. I like to imagine it was her way of saying, *Thank you for loving my mom as much as I do. And for doing things like this for her that I cannot do, because I do not have opposable thumbs.*

Even with this "wow this was very different from my experience with Rosemary" contrast, it still wasn't until months later, when she offered to take me out for my birthday, that I realized how right I was to feel concerned about my friendship with Rosemary.

I hadn't had much, if any, experience with birthday dinners personally, though I'd attended many and knew the hell of the split check where I got soup and everyone else got steak. And this wasn't going to be a group dinner, but that's still what I think of when I think of birthday dinners: Order as much as possible, because you'll all split the check and someone ordered lobster.

Two people had offered to take me for one this year, Rosemary and Audrey. I assumed both of these birthday celebrations (wow, two whole people!!!) would be very similar, but instead, it was like a children's parable about two extremes.

Rosemary's celebration was first. She took me to a restaurant that was pretty good but didn't have much I could eat. I often feel weirdly self-conscious about my myriad food allergies because Cool Girls eat steak and air and whiskey and never have autoimmune issues they did not at all choose, and she knew that. But still, maybe people make mistakes.

Rosemary offered to just get whatever I wanted and we'd share it, which I'd never really done, because the one thing I have in common with Joey from *Friends* is "Lane doesn't share food," which she might not have known, but I didn't feel comfortable telling her, in a bid to be "normal" (see: matching what anyone else wants to do).

I hate sharing food so much. Just give me my own food! I don't want to have to count how many bites I had, or how many poppers I already ate and how many you had, so we divide it up fairly. It's too much stress, get your own.

Rosemary asked me what else I wanted to do for my birthday, anything at all! But she didn't fully understand how, when you come from extreme denial of your own wants, you can become fully incapable of knowing what you want, and what your options are.

Because I'm still new to feeling that I'm allowed to need anything, and trusting that people who offer it really want to offer it, someone asking what I need often feels like they're asking me to order from a menu I've never seen before. What's on the menu? If it turns out it's a Thai restaurant and I need a Yankee candle, then I wasted both of our time, and I look like an idiot and now you're mad because I asked for a Yankee candle and you're a Thai restaurant. Ugh, OK fine, well then do you have any eye serums? No? Great, now I'm banned for life from this strip mall.

I'd spent so many years not having resources, or options, or choices, that I made myself OK with that, made myself smaller, so that reaching out and expanding still felt danger-ous, even when it was finally safe.

I told her a very abridged version of this, and she said, "Well, this dessert menu won't do, so we are getting you des-sert elsewhere if you want! I want you to have the best birth-day ever and I want to give you that!!!" Sadly, still battling a chronic case of "OMG you don't HAVE to" (which certainly wasn't helped by what happened with her months prior), I pushed it aside and said, "Maybe later!"

She had an idea. She took me to a bar (I don't drink) that only served chicken wings (I don't eat meat) so we could hang out (see also: I could drink water and watch her drink and eat wings)! What an awesome tailor-made option for me! I made the most of it, and to be fair, I couldn't think of what I wanted to do, so who was I to complain that this was wildly not it?

Later that night, Rosemary was kind of sloshed and we walked to this ice cream place and stood in line outside because I guess they were really busy. They were closing in twenty minutes, but surely, they would accommodate the existing line. During that twenty minutes, Rosemary said, "I wanted to give you the best birthday—did I do it? Did I give you the best birthday? I did it, right? I gave you the best birthday! I did that! I DID THAT FOR YOU! Right? I did, right?" And I kept wondering why I was spending my birthday watching her do what she wanted to do and appeasing her need to know she was a Great Friend, which seemingly eclipsed her desire to actually be one? No, that couldn't be it. I must be mistaken. She spent the rest of the twenty minutes asking me if she "looked fat" and if she was hot or not. And I spent the remainder of my birthday assuring her she was hot.

For bizarre reasons unknown to me and everyone else who was waiting, the ice cream shop did not accommodate the line. After twenty minutes, they took one more customer and told the rest of us to get fucked. Rosemary sweetly told them, "Please, it's my friend's birthday!" And I tried to wash away all of the weird "Wait, did you want to be a good friend to me, or just appear to be a good friend to me? Please tell me the latter is totally incorrect so I can just have friends already" feelings I was now flooded with, after ignoring them for so long.

And then I went home, without ice cream, without feeling taken care of, feeling like I'd done a great job on my birthday by making my friend feel good about herself, which I don't think is what a birthday is supposed to be about. I didn't realize how accurate that suspicion was until I met up with Audrey later that week, which I'll get to in a moment.

A few weeks after my Birthday Nightmare, Rosemary told me we were going to do Part 2 of my birthday, since "I told you I'd get you ice cream and I'm gonna get you ice cream!!!"

We did not get ice cream. Instead, we met up at a museum she'd wanted to go to, and I suddenly realized that Rosemary was someone who, if I ever mentioned anything painful or frustrating, she would stop talking to me, look away, and only listen to me again when I'd said something funny and light. As though my pain disgusted her and I was failing at my purpose, which was to entertain her. I would usually oblige, not fully conscious this was happening, but on this day, I finally saw it for what it was and I was furious. I was her pet monkey, her court jester. We weren't friends. I was the funny, weird girl, a stray she was generously taking in.

We went to get lunch together, at another place that was just fine, and she didn't pay for the museum or the lunch, so I have no idea how any of this was Birthday Part 2, but OK. After garbage lunch, she suggested I come over to her house because she had "some beautiful clothes I'm giving away that you'd *love*." We took a cab very far uptown to get them, after a long, exhausting day of feeling like her quirky purse dog. But maybe, just maybe, the clothes *were* great!

We got inside, and the clothes were . . . in tatters. Most were from an old boyfriend who just wore stained navy-blue T-shirts and beaten-up khakis. And if I picked up any items she had in there that were remotely nice, she would TAKE THEM BACK TO KEEP. Finally, she said, "Sorry I took everything you wanted and just kept it. I do have one dress you'd love though!" She brought the dress out. I was very, very tired by that point, so I started to put it in my tote to try on when I got home. She refused and said if I wanted to take it, I had to try it on in front of her, now. Too tired to think about how insane that was, I tried it on over my clothes. She said it was, "SO cute!!!" followed by the reveal that she was going to keep it for herself. I stared at her like she'd just told me she keeps dead bodies in the closet. As I went to the front door, the door to an escape from whatever this day had been, she said, "OH! And I didn't forget the ice cream. If you walk about eight blocks there's an ice cream place right there."

What, on earth, was this? Not wanting to walk another eight blocks to buy my own belated birthday ice cream, I just got on the train home and thought, *Hm, I feel like this friendship is really bad?* But how could that be? She wanted to be a great friend to me, she wanted to care for me. On paper this was a good friendship, so why wasn't it a good friendship in practice?

***

On the absolute other end was Audrey. Days after whatever Birthday Part 1 was, Audrey took me to one of my favorite restaurants, where everything is amazing, and used every second of our dinner together to make me feel loved and supported and special. The dinner was in no way a celebration of what a good friend she was, what a kind charity she was performing for an in-need stray. It was an active celebration, a celebration that I was born and that she got to know me.

I told Audrey what had happened with my surgery and Rosemary—tentatively, worried that I'd read it all wrong, that I was being too fussy, no one's perfect, it's OK. Audrey was livid at every part of it. Why hadn't she brought the snacks??? Why didn't she blow off work or reschedule it??? Why did she even come over if she was just going to use my apartment like a workspace and not be there for me after surgery??? Why even ask to take me out on my birthday if she wasn't going to do anything she said she'd do???

After a lifetime of asking myself these questions and immediately shutting myself up, I let Audrey's words in.

If you've never had true, good friends before, it is so easy to take whatever scraps someone is offering. An approximation of friendship. *Hey,* you think, *at least it's something.* Because you don't yet know what friendship should look like, should feel like. So when someone comes into your life, promising you many of the things you'd wanted and not delivering on them, you might think, *That's OK! No one's perfect and hey, someone verbally offering it is at least one step closer to getting everything I want.* But it is not.

If I hired you to work for me and I said I'd pay you $50,000, and then just never did, is that better than an unpaid internship, because at least I offered you payment? NO, IT'S NOT. And if anything, it's worse, because in the latter scenario, at least I told you what you were getting, and you could choose to be okay with that or not. But in the former scenario, you were outright lied to, to get you to take a job you wouldn't have otherwise accepted.

It's easy to see so many of these moments, these friendships, as people who chipped away at my hope for finding the friends I so deeply wanted and needed. But the closer I got to having the friends I wanted, the more I realized how useful these moments of disappointment actually can be. They're when I learned what's truly important to me in a friendship. What I'll no longer settle for. What I'll no longer accept. And what I can and should expect from others in the future.

And if you're finally seeing the flaws in your good-on-paper friends, and now striving for something more than that, let me tell you this: You don't want too many things. You want what you damn well want, which everyone is allowed. There is so much rhetoric I see, saying that you shouldn't "expect you from other people." That people are limited, and they can't be expected to give you as much as you give them. But it is so important to remember that you are very much allowed to require *you* from other people if that's what you need. If you give a lot emotionally, you are absolutely allowed to hold out for someone who can give the same amount of emotional resonance, the same amount of compassion, when they are able. And if someone sees those needs and knows they can't provide them, that's OK, too, but you're allowed to have them just the same.

If someone offers to take you out for dinner and ice cream, you damn well deserve someone who actually does that and then pays before you even see the check.

If consistency is important to you, crucial even, you *deserve people who do what they said they would do*. Because they know you need it. You deserve someone who makes sure they do the important things. Even if it's hard for them, because that's what people do when they love you.

You deserve people who check all your boxes, just as much as you check all of theirs. And it's OK to hold out until you find them. You will see this sentiment repeated throughout these pages, so please know that I am repeating it deliberately, because I often need to remind myself that I deserve them, and it's OK to need them, and it's OK to hold out for them, and maybe you need those continuous reminders as well.

As much as the world wants us to settle to just say we have friends, so we shouldn't overanalyze it, or want any more, it's vital to know that you're allowed to wholly disagree with that idea. Let them say what they want. If you need more, or want more, you can and should hold out for something that fits you better.

It isn't worth it to hold onto people who are kind of close to what you want but are also kind of harmful to you. And moreover, it doesn't serve either one of you.

I don't hate Rosemary, I really don't. I have compassion for whatever shaped her in this way, and maybe one day she'll see she had these patterns and heal, and we'll reconnect (I love a redemption story so much, and to a fault, like *please stop hoping they'll magically change, trauma brain, that never ends well*). And it's also OK if we don't. Because sometimes people come into our lives just to show us what we don't want, and those people have given us the gift of being a mirror. And that mirror shows us who we really are and all that we've buried, all the needs we've pushed underground because they seemed unsightly. And if we're lucky, another friend comes into the picture soon after, to confirm that the needs we've buried *can* be met, can rise from the earth like buds, to be watered, and nurtured by the people around us, until we see that our needs were not burdens, not unsightly flaws to be worked on, but instead, vital parts of us that deserve to bloom.

Good-on-paper friends are so seductive because we want to find our people so very much, so if someone walks up to us and says, "I'm your person! I'm here! I want to give you everything you want!" it's exhilarating and very tempting to believe them outright. Why would someone lie about that? And the truth is, I don't think most people do lie about it. I think most people who do this absolutely want to be able to give you what you need. But then as you get closer, you, or they, might realize they don't have what it takes, and they're not as suitable for the "position" as they thought they might be.

You only find out if a friendship works, if it has the potential to be real and true, by getting to know someone and seeing how they fit in your life and how you fit into theirs. By showing up for people and allowing them to show up for you. And then taking note of those moments when you didn't get what you needed, or are shrinking what you need in order to accommodate their limitations of what they can give.

And above all, by listening to that little voice in your head, or your heart, that says this friendship should work, you wish it would work, and yet it just doesn't. And then forgiving yourself for not seeing it sooner, because at least you're finally seeing it now, and you can take what you've learned and do better next time. And there is always a next time.

Learning Your (and Your Friends') Attachment Style

It's my responsibility as your best friend to make
sure you do exciting things, even when you don't
want to. —Sookie St. James, *Gilmore Girls*

Look, I love the "they're opposites, and they're best friends"
trope as much as the next consummate TV watcher. But a lot
of times when TV characters are opposites, a big part of how
they are opposites is their attachment style. This means "we
experience love in different ways, and we give and receive love
in different ways." While that can be great to watch, because
it's fictional and you never doubt they love each other, even if
they struggle to show it at times, if someone in your own life
receives and gives love in a radically different way than you do,
that can be incredibly stressful.

But we don't always see that in these depictions. We simply tell people opposites attract. Look at Jane and Petra on
Jane the Virgin, Khadijah and Max from *Living Single*, Rory
and Paris on *Gilmore Girls*, Carly and Sam from *iCarly*, Jen
and Judy from *Dead to Me*, Mary and Rhoda from *Mary Tyler
Moore*, Molly and Issa from *Insecure*, Nick and Schmidt from
New Girl, Jess and Nick from *New Girl*, Eleanor and Chidi
from *The Good Place*, Joan and Toni from *Girlfriends*, David

and Stevie on *Schitt's Creek*, Buffy and Willow from *Buffy the Vampire Slayer*, and Ryan and Seth from *The O.C.*

Opposites seemingly attract because there are learning opportunities there. Two opposites can balance each other out and open each other up to new things. This is the kind of friendship many people have, where someone is strong in the ways you are weak and vice versa, and you strengthen each other. How lovely is that, if that was always the only difference between you?

When we see opposite friends with potentially different attachment styles, they often bend easily to meet the other person's needs, and usually over one very special episode they'll address it and fix it in a clean thirty minutes. I've learned so much about attachment theory through my own experiences and research, and examining how it relates to all my relationships, *especially* my friendships, which often takes a lot longer than thirty minutes, commercials included.

Attachment theory is essentially an indicator of how easily you're able to attach or get close to other people, based on how easily and safely you were able to get close to people as a child. So if you had emotionally available, safe parents, you're more likely to have a "secure attachment" and be able to readily give and receive love without hesitation because you know it to be a safe thing to do (AKA the system is rigged, but I digress). But if your childhood was full of absent, unsafe, unavailable, or unreliable caregivers, having the ability to get close to people is often far more challenging.

Usually, those people will split off into two categories of insecure attachment styles: avoidant attachment, anxious attachment, or a combination of the two.

People with avoidant attachment styles want love and connection just as much as anyone else, and it's possible they fear it just as equally as anxious attachment styles do; however, they are much quicker to run and evade and find reasons to "get to safety." So if anxious attachments are always worried the avoidant is mad at them and going to leave them, the avoidant attachment interprets that as needy and annoying and uses it as a reason *to* leave them, since they already want to leave everyone all the time anyway, and that's a good enough reason as any. This often begs the question: If avoidant people want connection just as much, why do they often retreat when it arrives? And it's because they start to feel suffocated. They want closeness but usually once they actually start getting close to someone, they quickly feel like they're being trapped, so they can never truly have that closeness without doing deep work to untangle their correlation between "people who need things from them" and "people who are trying to bleed them dry."

Recently I realized that I, a person with an anxious attachment style (though throughout my life, I've had every insecure attachment style, and now have a partially secure attachment style, please clap), have so often attracted avoidant attachment friends. While these differing attachment style friends fit the "we're SO opposite" trope in a very delightful way, I was still entering into a friendship with someone who hated vulnerability and emotions, while I live for both, which would almost be comical if it wasn't so fraught.

Despite there being a mutual love and desire for your friendships to work, having clearly incompatible attachment styles between you can often be a huge harbinger of what you can and can't expect from your friends.

And while some people might find they pick friends with compatible attachment styles, but choose romantic partners with incompatible attachment styles, or vice versa, I'm (not at all) happy to report that I've often picked people with avoidant attachment styles as partners *and* friends. Please clap, and also pray, for me.

The worst part of this is that it can be really hard to tell what someone's attachment style is when you're just friends. It's so much easier to spot when you're dating someone because the intimacy is often more immediate, so you can fairly quickly see where someone stands. But we tend to "casually date" friends for a longer period of time without outlining expectations and commitments as clearly. We don't want to get too close just yet, since we don't know what the other person is looking for and we don't want to be needy. So we "see where it goes," not wanting to scare them off, or seem too intense. Because of that, it's possible, depending on the level of intimacy or how often you see them or speak with them, that you might not fully realize what a friend's attachment style is for years into the friendship. And if it turns out to be greatly incompatible with your own, well, what do you do now?

So many friendships require us to just wade farther and farther into the ocean, not knowing what's out there, how deep or shallow the water gets, if there's a sudden drop off, or if it's full of sharks—which I guess in this case are "fundamental incompatibilities with how deeply we're both willing and able to connect with each other." I can't even imagine that being a kind of Shark Week, too scary.

These incompatibilities can be worked through, yes, but the work required by both parties can be significant. Not only do you both need enough self-awareness to know how you connect with people, what your needs are, and how much you can give, but you also have to know whether or not you both have the tools and willingness to work through any rough spots.

Friendships really are the biggest group project you'll ever be a part of, and many people address friendships the same way they address group projects:

1. They opt out of doing any work, assuming the other person will do it.
2. They do all the work and resent everyone else for not doing their part.

I have often found myself in category two—in both group projects and many of my friendships.

Undoing that pattern requires a few things, chief among them, the ability to mitigate how much you give, to allow other people to give just as much as you do, and trusting they will, because you've finally chosen someone who is a good match for you.

Part of the problem here is we're told to find people who feel like home to us. And if your "home" was full of unhealthy patterns and toxic relationships, what will feel like home to you is actually the last place you should be.

You will often feel very comfortable with people who "feel like home" to you, but not in a good way. It's part of the raw deal you get when you didn't have that perfectly emotionally available, safe, loving family growing up: a whole lot of "just do this!" advice that absolutely does not apply to you.

So now, here you are, trying this idea on like a pair of shoes every other kid at school has, but they look awful on you and you're just trying to find a way to make them work so you can fit in. And it must be your fault somehow.

In more extreme scenarios, you think you have found that "home" feeling and, oops, now it's been a year and yeah, this is abusive as hell. And you couldn't see it, because it felt so destined, so perfect, so meant to be, so "right." Because, in a sad way, it did feel "right." You'd become so used to a very unhealthy expression of "love," whether it was enough for you to actually feel loved, or not. As a result, your feeling of home might actually be a warning sign, which is something it took me my entire life to learn.

In those cases, that friendship isn't destiny, or fate. Your "it just felt right" isn't a perfect friendship, it's a trauma bond. Your feeling of "I have to do whatever I can to make this work, even to my own detriment" isn't loyal friendship, it's a familiar dynamic, subconsciously keeping you tethered to this person who may not be good for you. If you'd been able to have healthier connections when your child brain was forming, you'd think, *Yeah this is too much work, pass,* or *We actually don't have that much fun, no thanks.* Friendship would mean trying each other on and seeing if it fits, instead of forcing a size 7 shoe onto your size 9 foot because you really want it to work, and you're already used to having to force painful shoes on your body, so hell yes! A perfect fit.

If you're in a friendship with someone who has a fairly incompatible attachment style with yours, that doesn't mean it can't work out, or that it's definitely a trauma bond. But I've noticed in my own experiences that many of my friendships are greatly at odds with aspects of my anxious attachment style.

This means, in the simplest terms, that I am often thinking, *Are you mad at me? Am I doing this friendship correctly? How can I subvert my needs to make you happy? I don't want you to think I have too many needs and then leave me. All that matters is that you do not leave me, not whether I actually like our friendship, because if you like me, then I can feel safe.* And my avoidant attachment friends are often thinking, *Please don't need anything more from me. Should I leave this friendship soon? It's easier to be alone. All that matters to me is that I can leave whenever I want and never get too close, so I can feel safe.* Neither one is right nor wrong, but you can see how that friendship would be extremely challenging to navigate for both parties.

But so many anxious attachments hurtle toward avoidant attachments, like a moth to a bright flame, because we *became* anxious by having caregivers who couldn't or wouldn't consistently love and care for us, and now here's this person who can't or won't consistently love and care for us? Cha-ching! (That's the sound of the cash register from hell.)

As soon as I learned about attachment styles, I looked at every past romantic relationship through the lens of what I'd learned, but I never looked at my past and present friendships through the exact same lens until somewhat recently. And once I did, I realized nearly every friend I'd ever had has avoidant attachment to a really obvious degree, if not every single one. I just didn't know about that yet, so I always chalked it up to "Ha ha opposites! We're cute!" which is true for some, but it's such a crucial lens to see things through if you're not getting everything you want out of good-on-paper friendships.

Your attachment styles will reveal the fundamentals that make a friendship either really strong, or something that you might never truly feel safe if they remain unaddressed. And then you can use that information to strengthen the friendships that feel like they just need a little adjustment, together. I want to highlight "together" with a million markers, because in most of my friendships, I thought that if I did all their homework for us both they'd love me. Wow, what an extra-credit-doing dream! But the truth is, no matter how hard you work, you can't assume that your "help" will ensure that someone else is willing and able to do that work on themselves, or that they're ready to yet. The idea that "people can only meet you as deeply as they've met themselves" is true.

You can't tell someone, "I think you're doing this, probably because of x trauma, so do this!" Even if your intent is to be helpful, they have to get there on their own. That's their path to explore and discover. And sometimes you're just further along in understanding your own needs and wants than your friend is right now. They may want your help in getting there, or they may not. These are all just pieces of information to notice. You can't always see that until you start to see the cracks in the relationship, which you can either brush off, or let them continue to fracture until it's in too many pieces to ignore.

* * *

In many of my friendships with people who have avoidant attachments, I've noticed there is a pattern of pushing and pulling, and it doesn't always begin the way you'd think. I've noticed many times avoidant attachments will begin a friendship with bold declarations of love, gifts, and promises that have, at times, resembled lovebombing (which is usually when a romantic interest showers you with love, almost to an over-whelming degree, as a way to get you into the relationship, only for those gestures to stop fully once you're in it).

Lovebombing is typically talked about as a manipulation tactic in romantic relationships, but some friendships I've had mirrored this exact practice in ways I've noticed only recently, though not necessarily with malicious intentions. And the hardest part of this is that unless you know for sure that some-one's intention is to manipulate you (would be a great cheat sheet to have), most people who do these grand declarations and showering of affection and then suddenly stop doing any-thing they'd promised at all, aren't doing it because this was some big con. They may have simply felt really excited about you, and genuinely wanted to keep doing them, but then later realized they couldn't.

Many avoidant attachments genuinely want to do the things they promise, genuinely mean the things they say, and then later scare themselves with how much they care for this new person, or tell themselves this person probably doesn't want the things they promised anyway, so why does it matter? The retreat into "I'm better off alone where I don't have to stress about getting close to someone" begins. And even out-side of attachment style, many people struggle with follow-through due to their own struggles they wish they could mag-ically fix, but they can't. That does happen. And in those cases, it's important to remember "it's not you, it's them," but since you can't know someone's secret reasons if they don't tell you, and the avoidant attachment is the least likely of all to tell you if and how they're hurting, all you know is they've made promises they're not keeping and it feels disappointing. And you have every right to be upset by that if it continues without explanation, or any signs this will change one day, especially if you're someone who needs consistency from people.

Lack of consistency and an unwillingness to talk about their emotions are hands down the biggest struggles I've had with my avoidant attachment friends. Often I'll find myself sensing they're upset about something and feeling like I have to find the right words to pry it out of them, to make them comfortable enough to tell me if they're upset, chase them when they run, and try not to feel hurt when they don't give a lot emotionally. And that push and pull begins.

Since I've had so many friendships where this pattern has come up, and it sounds very stressful, you might wonder what the upside of being friends with a conflicting attachment style would be, and the answer is two things: 1. They remind you of the toxic bonds you had with your caregivers, which feels "comfortable" to you, and 2. Sometimes even though your attachment styles are different, your love languages are spot on, and this combination creates something powerful right away. Many avoidant attachment friends I've known love to cook and I am truly a slut for anyone who feeds me. They've also loved to give gifts and I am similarly slutty for presents. 3. Sometimes you just really, really like this person because *a person is not their attachment style.*

The struggles tend to come from the trust you're able to find within the dynamic. As someone with an anxious attachment, I often have a hard time trusting there aren't any strings attached to someone's kindness, there isn't some trap door that I'm about to fall through because I "fell for it." And when that anxiety creeps in, the best thing you can do is to just continue to receive and give, trust and give it time, bit by bit. And bit by bit might turn into watching bad reality TV and having Cheesecake and Fries nights, where you just eat a whole cheesecake and waffle fries together in comfy clothes, and continue to hope for the best. And reminding yourself that when those insecurities come up, you might need reassurance, and hopefully they'll be open to providing it.

It's likely that if you're in a friendship like this right now, you already see a few warning signs that this friendship is going to be challenging, though I hesitate to call them that because they aren't always extreme in any way. Sometimes warning signs don't foretell doom exactly, as much as they tell you there are dynamics at play that need to be addressed, need to be clearly spoken about, and a mutual plan needs to be devised to make sure everyone feels good in this relationship despite them. But if you're not the type to bring that up, or aren't sure how to do it, or you worry if you bring it up they'll leave (anxious attachment) that dynamic festers, creating a rot that, if unaddressed, could kill the whole plant from the roots up.

And even if you do talk to them about what you need, and they hear you, and promise to work on it, they ultimately might not be able to give it to you. Not because they don't want to, not because they don't care, but because they are wired differently than you are. It's so much easier to think someone isn't meeting your needs because they don't care about you at all, they are just a bad person, end of story, than to realize someone wants to meet your needs but cannot.

It's brutal to hear that someone is unable to give you certain things that are so important to you, not because they don't want to, but because their brain struggles to do that, or because their past told them the only way for them to survive was to keep that part of themselves guarded, because of their own unhealed parts. How do you hold all the parts of that, the part that loves and accepts them with all their current limitations, but also might need a bit more from them, because of your own past, and your own unhealed parts? How do you ask for something that might be hard, or even painful, for them to give, and are you a bad person if you do that? You don't know, so you just try to work through it.

In the best cases, if both people can bend and find something in the middle that works for them, that can be the way forward and it is so beautiful when it's able to happen. But even with the best communication, an avoidant person might never understand why an anxious person needs so much reassurance when they pull away, and can't openly set boundaries or voice what they need, what they want and need, even if you explain to them that anxious attachments often can't do this because they feel like if they need anything, the other person won't like them and they'll leave, so they turn themselves into a T-shirt canon of giving. And anxious attachments may not be able to understand how avoidant attachments are able to so freely be themselves, take it or leave it, and set boundaries whenever they need to, even if they know it's because avoidant attachments aren't as afraid of having someone leave, they're far more afraid of being trapped or hurt again, so what's the worst that could happen if they set a boundary and the person doesn't like it? They're back to being alone, which feels so much safer to them anyway, win-win!

It can be hard for both of you to see that the other person's attachment style isn't a choice, any more than yours is. They can't magically be better at giving you what you need overnight, and you can't magically stop needing what you need overnight. And in these cases, the anxious attachment will often will buckle, and subvert their own needs to accommodate, so they don't lose their avoidant friend, despite their mounting concerns.

And one such concern that comes up for me often is friends who have a habit of frequently offering me something wonderful and then simply never doing it. And I'm not talking about people who occasionally forget and you just have to remind them because they're human and it happens, or people who tell you "Oh I totally forgot! I'll bring it Tuesday!" and then bring it Tuesday. I'm talking about people who constantly promise you something out of the blue, whether it's giving you a gift, or offering a big gesture, and you say "thank you so much!" and you feel that glow, and they feel that glow, and then they never do it, and you feel absolutely insane.

You feel like you can't bring it up, because it feels weird to be angry at someone for offering to do something lovely and then not following through. And it feels awful to have to send a "just circling back on this!" note to your friend who offered to do something nice for you, like now it's your job to make sure they do it?! A nightmare. So now you're mad, and you feel like you can't be mad, or shouldn't be mad, and then you're mad about that too.

Let me tell you something I wish I knew then: It's very OK to be mad about that! Extremely OK, regardless of their attachment style, regardless of their intentions. If this feels awful to you, and it happens all the time, and they know it bothers you, and you want more than apologies and a quick fix right now (see: "I'll do it Thursday and make it up to you!" and then the pattern begins again the next time), and you need to see long-term changes, or you don't want to be friends anymore? Fair. And it is far better than the alternative, which is to pretend it doesn't bother you, because you feel silly for being bothered by it. Which is what I often did.

You have to talk about it, even if that means they might leave, or it gets awkward, or worse. Sometimes when I'd been able to muster the courage to bring up things like this to my friends for the first time, or the fiftieth time, I'd get so nervous, and then they would listen, they would validate that they had done that, did do that, struggled to not do that, and it seemed so promising, and then ... they'd just continued to do it, sometimes even during the conversation itself.

There were so many times in my friendships where I thought the answer was to just give them more chances, ignore the building list of disappointments, and try to lessen how much I needed to accommodate what they were able to give. And I have since realized this is the absolute worst plan.

We tell people to fully love and accept someone with all their flaws, to love and accept the things they cannot change, and that is something I believed my whole life, and still believe, but now with the very firm caveat of ... *unless it is causing you pain.*

I never understood when people said you can't love someone else if you don't love yourself first. I was perfectly fine to love other people fully, while giving myself scraps, perfectly happy making sure other people's needs were consistently met, while mine were met "if they had time, no worries." But now I believe that phrase really means, "You have to choose yourself first for it to really be a healthy love." You have to make sure your needs are being met and theirs are too. Your own needs cannot and should not be an afterthought. And having total love and acceptance of people you're close to, while settling for the bare minimum, or less, from them will kill you every time.

So I'll encourage you to ask yourself, "What do I need from my friendships that is absolutely necessary to me to receive, regardless of how much I like them or how much we have in common? And which friendships do I have that are not meeting these needs, and have I communicated those needs before, and if I have, why am I OK with this person not meeting those needs?" When you finally realize the other person isn't willing or able to meet your needs, no matter how much you've tried to talk about it, the only thing you can do is to distance yourself for the moment, or leave altogether. And amidst your grief, you may find you need to unfollow, or even block them on everything, and it will feel *horrible*.

Before social media, you could take a break from a friendship, or stop being friends with someone and then not see them until you wanted to. It was painful, yes, but there were no extra steps you had to go through to part ways with them. You didn't have to drive to their house and draw an X on their mailbox so that they knew you fully hated them. You could just stop talking. Maybe you'd still see each other out and it was awkward, or, god forbid, you went to school together and you had to see them in the hallways. But you never had to think, *Do I remove this person who I once loved and who meant so much to me, on one, if not all, social media platforms? Is that childish? Is it necessary? Is it heartbreaking? Is it cruel? Or just a formality? Is it permanent or temporary?* And then cope with the act of actually doing it.

You know you've only done this because it just wasn't working, and the pain is so great, and the grieving needs to begin, and you need them digitally *gone*. At least for now. But any time I've had to do this, I still worried I would really hurt them by blocking them, despite telling myself this wasn't designed to hurt them, and that wasn't my intention. The fact was I couldn't look at this person who I felt knew what I needed and wouldn't give it to me, couldn't give it to me, at least not now, possibly not ever. Reminding me, sharply, of people from my childhood who knew what I needed and would not give it to me either. And finally setting even this one boundary with them, in any way, felt like death. The love was still there, those feelings and those memories remained, but now that I'd faced how this friendship is impacting me, I couldn't run from it anymore. You can't help what you need.

I think more than anything, many of my avoidant friends and I would've been perfect coworkers, perfect casual friends, perfect sometimes friends. But so often the good is so good with them, that you hang out more, talk to each other more. And the closer you get to each other, the more you realize what you'd need from them if that is the case. I can't tell you how many times I've had someone with an avoidant attachment tell me I am one of their best friends, and I was very confused, my first thought was, *Really? I made the cut?* and my second was, *But why is it that I don't always feel that closeness, that safety, with you?*

I just always assumed that when you were best friends with someone, you both got what you needed most of the time. No one secretly felt drained and a little shortchanged, on an endless seesaw, seemingly out of their control and fully under the control of the other person.

When we see opposites attract friendships on TV, they may be opposites on the surface, yes, but I've noticed that when you look closer, they're often extremely similar at their cores. And that's why we see them easily bend to meet the other where they're at: because they have to, or the fictional friendship won't work. In real life, however, it's often not that simple.

In many of my own friendships like this, I had taken a very guarded, "It's my way or nothing" person and a people-pleaser and tried to make them best friends. And so OF COURSE the more guarded one will have an easier time feeling close to the other person, and of course the people-pleaser will feel like *Uh, I do not love this personally?* It's a rough combination that requires a lot of awareness on both sides, and the ability to be fully yourself instead of contorting to who you think they want you to be. So when these friends told me they felt extremely close to me, I was surprised because what I was getting from them felt more akin to what I'd have with a casual friend. And in those moments, you feel so confused, and a little cheated. They're getting everything they want, and gushing about it, while you're feeling left out because they know your needs and boundaries and don't seem to be as mindful of them, or worry if they cross them.

Ideally someone would tell you, "You're one of my closest friends, you're like family to me!" and you would say, "Aw me too!" But if your first instinct is to say "Wait, really?" that may be a good indicator that this friendship isn't necessarily healthy.

Adult friendships should be about finally getting to know someone as the person you truly are and the person they truly are and all the people you'll become over the course of your friendship. It should not be about spending all your time trying to make yourself smaller and lesser, or making yourself chooseable, or what they want you to be, you did that enough as a teenager. Adult friendships should be all the more meaningful because you're *finally* being chosen for all the parts of you, needs included, that are now safe to share. And if you thought this friendship was going to be like that, and it isn't, forgive yourself for not knowing that.

You don't always know when you're overestimating how deep a friendship can go, or is meant to go, until you try. In romantic relationships, we often assume that if a relationship is really truly good, it's meant to last for the rest of our lives, it's meant to be The One. And if it's anything less than that, it's a failure. And we do this with friends a lot of the time as well. "This is going so well, and it's blossoming into something very close to what I want, so I'll go along with it and see what happens!" while not always seeing, or wanting to see, the ways that the friendship might not be able to maintain that particular dynamic. Maybe some of our friendships, even the ones that are beautiful and meaningful in so many ways, just weren't built for longevity, the same way you can't ask a parasol to withstand a hailstorm. A parasol may look very similar to an umbrella, it may double as one in a light rain, but for the most part, parasols are built for sunny days, shielding you just enough from the heat and nothing more. Any more pressure than that and it will fall apart, whether it wanted to or not, whether you hoped it would or not.

And if it does, you're allowed to want a friendship to be able to give you everything you need, even if they don't understand those needs because their needs are different. You're allowed to hold out for someone who can meet you where you're at. And to grieve all the broken parasols you lost along the way.

How to Identify and
Ask for What You Need

At least one person wants to help you, they do, they do.
—It Was Romance, "If You Need Anything Call Me"

Years ago, before my band It Was Romance formed, I was playing music with a guitarist and a drummer every week, and my drummer got into a minor car wreck. My guitarist at the time, Evan, immediately called me and said, "We have to go help him! Let's buy him drinks and food and show him we're there for him!" I was, of course, on board with helping him, and he was also swiftly attended to by his family, his partner, and a ton of friends who rallied. During that same period, I was in a deep mental health crisis that was increasingly apparent in rehearsals, but no one ever said, "We have to help her." At most I would hear, "If you need anything, call me."

I have always hated that phrase.

To me, it puts the onus on the person in pain to have the emotional energy, time, feelings of worthiness, and knowledge of what they need to ask for it—which I, rarely, if ever, have had all at the same time. In so many of my past friendships, I have engaged in a challenging dynamic of figuring out what is OK to need and what is OK to ask for. Am I explaining my needs clearly? Are my needs not being met because this person is unwilling to or incapable of meeting them, or are they capable of working with me to meet my needs but I am just not communicating them in a way they can hear them? And if I'm not, how do I find the language to do that?

What is reasonable to expect from a friend, especially one you see often, and how are you supposed to know the answer if you didn't get what you needed from your family or past friends either? It's possible you don't even know the options, and what if you need too much, and the fear of rejection keeps you from seeking friendships that you dream of?

It's that menu you've never seen before all over again. I know for some people it would be easy to answer. "I'd like you to listen," or "I want to pet a puppy, please find me a puppy," but it's not always easy to get to the point where you know what you need and are able to ask for it without fearing that someone will get angry at you for asking for the wrong kinds of comfort.

What are you allowed to need? And it varies from person to person, so it can feel scary to say, "Can you come over and braid my hair?" if all they wanted to offer was to buy you a beer. Do people in your life disappoint you because they're not good people, or do they disappoint you because you can't ask for what you need in a way where they can hear you? You don't know the answer, and then your resentment builds, both for their not intuitively knowing what you need, and for yourself, for not being able to articulate what you need and how to ask for it. Similarly, do they wish they didn't disappoint you and hate that they did, but the things you need are outside the scope of what they can offer you and they're not sure how to handle that? It's heartbreaking work to do and exhausting to navigate. And why can't people just be like they are in the movies, dammit? But let's go back to the guitarist.

Evan and I got along extremely well, as long as it didn't extend into any deep, emotional territory. We played so well together, had so much fun, and genuinely adored each other, but then there was an invisible threshold that was crossed where his ability to care about me seemed to end. The threshold seemed to be "whenever I talked about anything deeper than polite topics you'd discuss at a water cooler." Because of that, I assumed maybe he wasn't the type of person who was there for people if they needed help, but I still kept hoping I was wrong, and he would notice what I was going through, that someone would see the signs. Whenever someone says, "She's just doing that for attention" or "It's just a cry for help," it's like, yeah, so where is my attention? Where is my help? I don't know how either of those terms became something that we use to demonize and further neglect someone who is acting out of such desperation because they feel they are not being heard in the first place.

I'd seen so many movies about musicians watching a bandmate go through addiction or depression and helping them through it. I remember reading Hayley Williams say that talking to her guitarist, Taylor York, when she was facing hard times is what kept her going during that time. You're supposed to be a family, always having one another's backs, and I wanted that so much. But my experience here was very much "leave your issues at the door." At one point I even wrote a song about this exact situation, using what I thought were obvious references to this dynamic, both with them and just so many other people in my life at that time, thinking they would finally hear me and think, "Wow, this person really needs help, and made this great pop song about it." But all they seemingly thought was, *What a great pop song! Let's play it!*

I told myself that maybe I hadn't conveyed how bad things were, even though I had expressly told them, and told myself maybe they just weren't people who cared that much or took care of people in that way. "No big deal!" Until my drummer's accident, when Evan immediately sprang into action with "We must help him in the following ways."

I was so heartbroken to know this existed, for this person with a mildly bruised arm who had been vocal about how minor the incident was, but not for someone who was fighting a mental battle for their own life. After a few weeks of internalizing these feelings, I asked Evan outright why it had been so easy for him to do that for our drummer, but every time I came to him needing help, feeling so alone, he would say nothing.

I've been told that I tend to whisper when I need help, and it takes everything in me to muster a whisper, so much so that to me, it feels like shouting. But I know that unfortunately it is often imperceptible to others. And since I assume they can see me using all my courage and energy to finally shout what I need, over and over again, they must be ignoring me, fully able to hear me and choosing not to—when, in fact, it turns out they never even heard me open my mouth.

I have such vivid memories of being a teenager and trying to find a funny, casual way to tell people around me that I was struggling, so they didn't feel like I was burdening them. Tragically, the way I'd tell them was almost always *too* funny, so they never noticed, and the worst part is I *still do this*! And I just hope people see through it, and feel hopeless when they invariably do not.

In this case, Evan told me that it's easy to know what to offer when someone has a minor injury: Buy them a beer, bring a casserole, done. But when someone is dealing with something more complex, more nuanced, something you can't easily see on an X-ray, it's harder to know what they might need, so you just do nothing.

I've seen this many times. When friends can't see any visible injuries, they aren't sure how to help, especially when you're dealing with something that we don't talk about as a society that often. And knowing that, hearing Evan say it, didn't make the experience any less isolating. I'd explained to him that, for me, the cure is the same, it can still be buying me a drink or snacks or just listening. To make someone feel cared for, to show up. And it was so painful to tell him that and *still* not see him do any of those things. And then a few months later, in the final moments of our friendship, he told me that my struggles felt like an annoyance to him; a knife in the gut, a worst fear realized.

The way we handle or ignore other people's pain seems like an extension of asking someone how their day is going. We all know the correct response to that question is "Good, you?" even if that is not the true response. So much of puritanical culture is platitudes and politeness, surface-level interest and investment. "Oh no, someone broke their arm! Send a card and call it a day! You can now say you did something! You helped. What a great person you are. Yay, you!"

But what if something deeper is happening? Something messier, more emotional, less easy to solve with a grocery store cake and a bear balloon you picked up on the way home? Well, there's a very simple solution here, and the answer is to do nothing and imply the person should get a therapist because you're staying out of this one. "Figure it out, buddy. Best of luck!" Never mind that it can take many tries to find a therapist who is the right fit, it's costly, and the fact that your friendships should be able to at least provide basic empathy and a safe place for you to share what's really going on with you.

Obviously, in many cases, all someone is equipped to do is listen, but there's still an active way to listen, an empathic way to listen that feels heartier than dead silence, which can make the other person feel like they should stop talking ASAP because they're weirding you out.

Years later, I ran into Evan at a coffee shop where I was sitting and writing my first book. He was sitting right next to me, and I was very nervous that it might be as awkward for him as it was for me. But he was warm and older, and I was very open to the idea of getting that rare thing in friendship breakups, or breakups of any kind: closure. We did some polite chatting and then he said, "Hey, I just wanted to tell you, I've thought a lot about the way I treated you back then, and I'm sorry. You really needed someone, and I wasn't there for you and then treated you poorly." I remember it being simple, earnest, and rare, because it does feel rare for someone who hurt you to reflect and say, "Wow, I was at fault here and I regret it." Even if it took years, it's never too late to hear someone say they wish they'd done better by you. It was so deeply healing and appreciated, and while it should be the bare minimum, for so many of us, it's a revelation.

We rarely speak of how painful it can be to try to find someone who can be there for you, no matter what your struggles are. And how right we are to be frustrated by the moments in our lives when we weren't fully supported or seen by past or present friends.

Very often in depictions of friends in media, the problems people share are fairly common and simplistic: help with a breakup, help with a routine fight between usually loving relatives, asking for a raise at work, the death of a loved one. We have covered these bases, and typically we go no further than that. But beyond those depictions, we're only able to observe the models of friendship that our peers, parents, and siblings are experiencing around us, and it's hard to gauge what's really going on with them, because we're still very much on the outside looking in. So much of what we need to learn about friendships is experienced, and we're rarely taught how to navigate them past "I like them and they like me, we are friends, no other issues could possibly exist!"

That means we have largely taught people how to be friends in these limited scenarios only, and have left an impression that there is no template for how to be a good friend in any other scenarios—or worse, we've communicated to people that the more complicated, painful things in life are best kept inside you, locked away from the people who are supposed to be your backup.

And if you are someone who is struggling with your mental health, you may not be capable of reaching out, or don't know how to reach out, or don't know whether it is safe to reach out this time.

When people hear someone died by suicide, they often assume that person should've reached out, and why didn't they? But it's not that simple. We can't create a culture where it's not OK to speak about anything "scary" or overwhelming, even to ourselves, let alone someone else, and then wonder why we are losing people to mental health issues. We cannot continue to make islands of people because we don't know how to do any more than this, and then tell people who need more that they should "take it somewhere else."

We cannot continuously wonder, with each passing suicide, why the person "didn't say anything," when in some cases, it's likely they tried and weren't heard and/or simply felt they couldn't try anymore.

I've seen some people say things like "Your friends are not your therapist." And yes, it is important to make sure there is a reasonable expectation of emotional labor we can expect from friends depending on their comfort level—which you can only know by asking them what they can handle, what is out of their depth, and what space they can hold for you. That said, if they ask if you're OK, they should be prepared for you to say no, and be prepared to hold space for the reason for that no. Again, it's so crucial that both people are feeling cared for and that no one is helping at the expense of their own mental and emotional well-being. But in the wrong hands, the phrase "Your friends are not your therapist" could send the wrong message to someone in need.

Similarly, it's not necessarily "trauma-dumping" if you're asking someone to hold space for you and you've asked for their boundaries: It's sharing and reaching out for support. It is more likely to be trauma-dumping if you've started talking about personal traumas with someone you don't know well, or they weren't given the space to say they didn't feel comfortable hearing about that, or didn't have the energy at the moment. You need to proceed with caution and thoughtfulness in these cases, of course. And it's always an option to preface talking about these things with your friends by saying, "Hey, do you have space/time to talk about _____" if you know it might be hard for them.

But by and large, we do not need to reinforce, even accidentally, the idea that friendships are not the place to go with
anything real and you should strictly save all that for your therapist, whom you may or may not have. Especially when some
of those friends might very much want to help, but you're not
sure how to ask for it.

People who are struggling are so often told that it's their
responsibility to "reach out to someone." That advice is,
frankly, bullshit. The reason it is bullshit is that so often when
that person did reach out to someone in the past, that person
reacted in a harmful way (it's important to emphasize that this
is usually because we live in a society that has largely failed to
appropriately educate people on how to handle these situations, rather than an indictment of that person specifically),
thereby causing the person to think that reaching out to people is bad. This is doubly true if that person was also raised
in a household where they frequently asked for help, only to
be dismissed, belittled, or ignored altogether. Rightly, they're
going to cope by no longer reaching out.

So if you find yourself wondering whether you should
reach out to someone because they might need help, but
you're not sure, that's completely understandable. If someone
is really good at masking what's truly going on, and you genuinely had no idea, that's out of your control. And because
we're so socialized to ask, "How are you?" and reply, "Good.
You?" and move on, we're encouraged to not talk about what's
really going on, even if someone does want to know. Which
is why I always like saying, "How are you? And absolutely be
honest, how are you?" Because some people (myself included)
often need the reminder to break out of the cycle of "Good!
You?" and they need to know that, in this moment, it's safe to

really be honest. Which, again, should mean you're presently able to really hear that answer and show up for that person. There's nothing more painful than having someone say they really want to know if you're OK, and you take the energy to tell them you're not, and then receiving a gut-wrenching response. These reactions could include:

- Saying nothing at all.
- Changing the subject altogether, or making it about them.
- Telling you not to feel that way because "You're great!" or reminding you of all the reasons you shouldn't feel that way.

Again, these responses aren't terrible because they're malicious, but they feel terrible to someone who almost didn't reach out at all, but bravely did anyway, and now you're talking about your new Jeep. All that said, I'm obviously not a doctor. But I am a person with an entirely too lengthy history of dealing with mental health struggles in myself and the people I love, so I can tell you that all of those things are incredibly painful to hear.

And if you're not sure what to look for in terms of "warning signs," it can be as simple as seeing a friend feeling hopeless, losing interest in things they usually love to do, really struggling in a few areas of life, "joking" about wanting to give up, or feeling like everything is just intolerable. So many of us were taught to couch our true feelings in jokes or lighthearted sentiments that it can just be a matter of checking in to make sure the jokes are really just jokes, and trusting your gut when you see warning signs, even if someone says they're fine.

Of course, if you don't handle things perfectly and your friend does end up hurting themselves or getting worse, it is never your fault. And even if you do all of the following things, your friend will probably still need to work through a lot. But saying the right things instead of the wrong things can make a hell of a difference.

So here are some things you can do when your friend really seems to be struggling:

1. **Tell them you are so sorry they're hurting this much.** Many people who are really struggling with their mental health feel like others do not understand the gravity of the situation or the immense, unbearable amount of pain they might be in. Tell them you hear them, you see it, and you are sorry they're going through this.

2. **Offer to come over and hang out with them.** When I was really struggling, I can't tell you how many times I just wanted someone to come over and sit next to me. We didn't even have to do anything. I just wanted them there. So, offer to do that.

3. **Bring them something small that shows you're thinking of them.** If you know they're having a hard time, next time you see them, bring their favorite juice or a smoothie or a soda or a key ring with something you know they love on it. Remind them there are still good things in the world and you care.

4. **If you have no idea what they're going through, you don't need to pretend you do.** If you've had similar mental health struggles, that can often be really helpful for someone to hear. But often when someone's going through something painful, people are tempted to say, "I know exactly what you're going through!" when it might not be similar at all. I would, in general, steer clear of "I

know exactly what you're going through!" unless you're absolutely sure the situation and the emotions are exactly the same, which they so rarely are.

5. **Tell them you have no idea what to say.** Don't know what to say? That's OK! But saying, "I don't know what to say" is way better than fumbling for a joke, or making a quick subject change, or not saying anything at all, all of which can be hurtful. Maybe you don't need to say anything anyway. Maybe you just need to listen. And bring cupcakes. Lots and lots of cupcakes.

6. **Ask if they have a therapist, or a good support system.** Maybe they've already told their therapist about struggling with this, but maybe not. Maybe their therapist is not that great. Maybe they're working on it, but it's still hard. Maybe they don't have a therapist and you can help them find one. Whatever the case may be, ask! But also, make it clear you're still there to talk and not just passing them off to a therapist, or another person who may not exist.

Some people might argue that it's not "their job" to help someone in these instances, and to that I say this: Friendship is entirely voluntary, and there is a sort of "terms and conditions" that comes with it, and you get to decide on those together, of course. And yes, if the friendship is no longer serving you, you can unsubscribe! You can move on. But when people have made you feel like they only like you when you're happy (or pretending to be), and that your pain is annoying to them, and they don't know why you're bothering them with it, it's absolutely OK to say, "Uh, it was pretty reasonable to assume that someone who calls me a close friend and says they love me would want to help me out in a time of need? But OK, guess this friendship is not for me!" And yeah, sometimes it's inconvenient! Or costly—mentally, emotionally, physically, or even financially. But that's why you communicate, that's why you get to say what you need, and ask what they can give. Like all relationships, friendship is an ongoing negotiation.

You don't need to be a medical professional to show up for someone, contrary to what I think a lot of people have internalized. So if you are someone who cares and wants to help a friend, I think we need to stop leading with "I don't think I'm the right person to talk to about this" as our go-to opening statement. For so many reasons. For one, if you start by saying what you *can't* do, the other person could feel like they are putting you out (which they probably already feared when asking for help). Instead, lead with the positive. The "right person" can be anyone, and it really depends on what the person says they need.

So before you dive in with caveats, listen. Hear what your friend is going through and assess what you could personally offer to help them, even if it seems negligible to you. You can say something like, "I'm so sorry to hear that. I'd be happy to come over with food, or keep listening, or make some calls for you for additional resources, since that can be overwhelming. Is any of that helpful?" And even if they say no, you have taken the initiative in a way that shows you are there, you do care, and are offering all the ways you could possibly help.

Similarly, sometimes someone might come to you needing help, but you're in a place where you need help, too. That happens so often with my friends and I, and when it does, it's OK to tell them that you're underwater right now too, and you wish you could do more, but you love them and you hear them. And then you can always try to do more for them when you feel better. Either way, an active response is still so much better than "Ugh, that sucks, dude" and moving on.

The only way for us to move away from a culture that stigmatizes mental health issues is to reach out if it seems like someone you love is struggling and you have the space to show up for them.

We have to support each other, and it has to be proactive. It has to fly in the face of the limited, archaic things we've been told about how involved it's OK to be, or how much it's OK to need. We need to start actively showing each other what we can give, and practicing how we can receive.

So often it can seem like life would be so much easier if people didn't need each other, or if everyone could just ask for what they need in a way we can hear, or if everyone could just intuit what we need so we don't have to say it. It's so easy to think people are islands, and anyone who gets stranded on another island did something wrong, or they should reach out to the other support systems they may or may not have, because we "shouldn't have to" take care of them. And that is all the more reason we should choose the friendships we cultivate carefully, so that if someone we've chosen, someone we love, is more isolated than we knew and doesn't have anyone but us, we will see this as a gift, an opportunity to be the person who finally shows up. To see their SOS and finally answer the call, ideally, before they even have to make it.

What to Do If You're in Love with Your Friend

> Harry: It only took three months.
> Sally: Twelve years and three months.
> —*When Harry Met Sally*

Like anyone who appreciates fine cinema, I have been deeply influenced by *When Harry Met Sally*. For many of us, this movie was the blueprint for "Oh yeah, we were just friends who never ever thought about having sex. Never! He was like a brother to me! And then one day I was like oh wait am I . . . in love???? With YOU? So weird!" which blows my mind on every level, since I've imagined falling in love with pretty much everyone I've ever met (because what if I didn't think about them being my soulmate, and then had to spend years inside a montage realizing it? No way. I wanted to skip to the good parts, thanks! Must consider all options, always).

The allure of the will they/won't they friends like Ross and Rachel from *Friends*, Nick and Jess from *New Girl*, Monica and Chandler from *Friends*, Dana and Alice from *The L Word*, Robbie and Julia in *The Wedding Singer*, Idgie and Ruth from *Fried Green Tomatoes*, Cher and Josh in *Clueless* (remember when it was a full goal to have a hot stepbrother to fall in love with? I'm still chasing that high), and Luke and Lorelai in *Gilmore Girls*, was that they truly got to have it all: a close, deep friendship that saw them through many life changes, a place to fall when romantic relationships didn't work out the way they'd hoped, a backup plan, even if only subconsciously, of someone who always loved them, whether it evolved physically or not. To hear pop culture tell it, you were supposed to be someone's best friend and then ignore the romantic chemistry until it got too much for one or both of you to handle. And then you either date and fall in love, or you date and it's a mess and you go back to being friends, only to end up getting married a few years down the line once you've both grown and/or it was the series finale.

So let's explore this idea that being a woman with a hot male best friend is extremely ideal. (This could also stand for any gender attracted to anyone, but for some reason the media really loves only showing straight people who are friends who secretly want to french. Wonder why that could be!) Despite the promises of a million romantic comedies that make it sound foolproof, the reality can be . . . less than that, in the following ways:

1. **"He will give you guy advice!"** I don't know why we have been told that having male friends means they can universally explain the inner workings of men they have never met, but the truth is people are complex and no one makes sense a hundred percent of the time.

2. **"Men are so much 'less drama.'"** The myth that "being friends with girls always leads to drama" is well-packaged sexism at its finest. Men get moody and weird and jealous and competitive and selfish just as much as women do. We can all be vulnerable, weird, petty people, and there is no gendered cheat code for this.

3. **"Maybe if we start out as friends, one day we'll end up together!"** There are so many movies about this, so many, so why wouldn't you want that? And while that is very possible, and has happened to some people (lightning strikes sometimes!), that doesn't mean it's that clear-cut every single time.

The truth is there is no "this will definitely work out great" configuration of this trope in the real world, but it's still something so many of us dream of. Because if it works out, you get so much good.

You get to start years into a relationship with them, because they already know your past and your exes, and you know their exes, their past. You know how to be better for each other because you know what didn't work in your past relationships. They already know your insecurities and all the things that made you who you are. And so you don't have to relay painful memories for the first time when things come up that make you anxious. You get the freedom of not having to wait to be your true self around them because they've known that beautiful weirdo for years already and they're still here, which is so powerful. And you don't have to get nervous about meeting their friends or their parents because you probably already know all those people and they love you and you love them.

And because all of that sounds like the absolute dream, even if we know we have a slim shot at realizing it, when it seemingly comes to us, we have to at least try.

And it seemingly came to me when I met Logan.

In many relationships from my past, I would always choose one friend to go to for anything I needed. And if I lost them, I felt like I died. I've read that this is super common with people who've been hurt a lot: You fixate on one person who feels safe, because you can't handle assessing the safety of multiple people. We talk about the dangers of doing this with romantic partners, the pitfalls of dating someone and then no longer talking to your friends and just focusing on them. We tell people this is bad because what if you break up? You won't have any friends left and you'll have no one. And this is also extremely true for friendships.

Logan became that friend. And because I am a Cool Loner who lives mostly in my head, of course we met online. He followed me on Twitter, and I saw he was a comedy writer who'd liked a lot of my posts, so I'd looked up some of his stuff and thought he was funny: truly the basis of most internet friendships. "You like a lot of my stuff, I like your stuff, too, we are friends now!" I DM'd him and told him we had some mutual friends, and we bantered a bit, before he switched us over to an email with the subject line "the great wild west of character limits."

His emails were funny and personal, and he included references that subtly let me know he'd looked me up by asking questions about my band and my writing, and he always ended his emails with "(1317 characters)," the number of characters over Twitter's rigorous limits.

It was that type of friendship where you're not sure if you're becoming best friends or falling in love or both. But you're hoping for the former one first and foremost, and ideally the second and third happen soon after, win-win.

I'm sure most people would choose falling in love with someone over platonic friendship, but for me? Hell no. Yes, I'm a romantic and I'd often loved to have things end up that way, but at the same time, falling in love with someone I was just becoming friends with was more anxiety provoking because it felt like that made it more delicate, more likely to end. But if I just stayed friends with someone, it seemed more likely it could last forever, or at least lay a firmer foundation for love several years down the line. And I would much rather have a lifelong, enduring friendship that involves occasional yearning than go all in on something that never should've been a romance at all and now you just hate each other and dodge each other on the street. To me, friendships have a better shot long-term, even if they are with people you sometimes want to make out with.

I had some reservations the first night Logan and I hung out, mainly because I noticed his comedy ideas were playful and silly "what if aliens hung out?" and mine were cathartic and urgent "what if women got to talk about trauma and then trauma stopped happening?" It frustrated me that so many men are allowed to think of silly weird things, while many of us are just trying to sort out the traumas of our lives so we have the mental space to think of things like *What if bread was your best friend on the moon?* But it was balanced by the fact that he knew I loved Stevie Nicks, and he learned "Landslide" on guitar so I could sing it while he played, and he was also allergic to gluten and bought us some really good cookies. Make music with me and provide snacks? I'm in.

Over the next few months, we became the best friends of my dreams. We hung out almost every day (I don't want to brag, but it was also *in person*) and wrote funny sketches. He brought me food when he came over, and we'd dogsit my friends' dogs together. It would've kept going on like this, except for two things that happened quickly after take-off:

1) I was pretty sure we were in love with each other and not talking about it, and we needed to talk about it, and 2) he got a job in LA.

The first one came to a head at a friend's karaoke party, which I had asked Logan to go to with me. He chose several songs for us to sing together: "Time After Time," "God Only Knows," and some other song in the same vein as "you're everything to me and I definitely love you and these would be a little weird to sing together if we were just platonic non-sexual pals."

Everyone at the party looked at us in that way—like we were a cute couple, but nope, we were Best Friends.

It was at that party, and with those song choices, that I realized I had to say something. Seeing people's faces being like *Aw what a cute couple who is definitely frenching* held a mirror up to the reality that we were at that very sweet part of the romantic comedy where you're like "Do we love each other?" This was Harry and Sally, except we were at the awkward part when they have to either put it on the backburner and start dating other people, or admit they like each other and finally pursue that. So, at the end of the karaoke night, after we'd both gone home, I called him on the phone. Even now, I can remember the feeling vividly.

I was pacing around my room, not wanting to ruin things but not wanting to deny them either. And I did this by saying the following: "Hey! So, I want to say something, and if I'm wrong it's totally OK, but I feel like I'm not wrong, and I just wanted to put it out there so we can talk about it, whatever it is. And again, if I'm wrong, it's totally OK." He laughed and said, "Sure, what's up?" and I said, "It just feels like we kind of like each other? Because it would greatly *appear* as though we're into each other. And again, if I'm wrong, it's cool. I just notice it a lot and a lot of people noticed it tonight so I figured, screw it. Let's talk about it."

He laughed and said, "Totally. I have thought about it a lot! But here's the thing: I always ruin everything with people. My longest romantic relationship has been one month. One month! I just tend to ruin things after that, or they get ruined. And when that relationship ended, I was so upset, and I just know I'd ruin things with you. And so, while I do have those feelings, very much so, it's not worth it to cross that line and maybe lose someone who's this important to me." And I said something appeasing like "Totally! For sure. I get it!" when what I wanted to say was, "Oh my god, you love me??? I will wait for you. Also, why are you treating me like a girlfriend if I'm not your girlfriend? This is an issue we should fix. Again, just in the meantime, until you go to therapy or get a brain transplant and realize you're brave enough to love again. Let me know!"

But in my heart, I knew this meant I had to set some boundaries. I couldn't look at him like a boyfriend, he couldn't treat me like a girlfriend. This wasn't a best friendship "and more" like in the movies. This was *When Harry Met Sally*, but still in the first half, when Harry was twenty-six and scared, instead of the third act, when he's thirty-something and finally ready. And before I could begin to parse what this new friendship reality would look like and how to put those feelings away even though they were, in the words of Sally Albright, "already out there," Logan got the job in LA. I was devastated.

I remember attending his going away party not long after our "Do You Like Me?" phone call and sitting there, psychically introducing myself to everyone there as, *Hi! I'm Lane.*

Logan told me if he was going to be with anyone it would be me, I'm basically his girlfriend, we're very in love. I'm his best friend. I'm sure you can tell! But I was just his friend. One of many. And seeing other women there, I wondered if he had that with all of them too.

The evening had that weird, scattered energy of going to a party with your Best Friend, where you don't know any of their other friends because you've created this bubble where it's only the two of you, and now they're suddenly hosting the party, and you're seeing them as someone else's friend for the first time.

You arrived in the bubble because you wanted it to be just the two of you, like best friends. Best friends who are falling in love. Which is a great way to realize you have very little idea of how this person acts when it's not just the two of you, which is probably a good thing to know about a person, especially one you're falling for. And now it's no longer just you two. It's now you, at a party, where it is them plus everyone and you are also there. And it shouldn't feel awful, but it does.

When we parted ways that night, other people were there too so we didn't get the goodbye I'd wanted: both of us crying, hugging each other like our lives depended on it, commemorating all we had and all that was to come, even though we'd soon be farther apart than we'd like. Instead, we got the goodbye you give at a big party where other guests are still there: "So good seeing you, have a good night!" I walked home and I cried the whole way, wiping tears away, like I'd just lost my best friend, or my boyfriend, or none of those things and I'd somehow imagined it all. And nothing could replace all the space that he'd created in my heart, which was now just an empty room that echoed when I spoke.

I suppose I could've kept the friendship with Logan long distance, but it didn't feel like I could at the time. I didn't want to take what was finally an in-real-life best friendship and turn it into a long distance one, especially when I kind of loved him, in whatever way, so deeply now. He never said, "Don't worry, Lane, we'll still be best friends who are in love with each other!" or "I'll call you every night!" He was just leaving, and it seemed implied that he was still technically there if I needed anything, but what we had when he lived nearby was gone.

In the weeks that followed I was grieving more than I knew, and I let myself fall into a pit of self-destruction and exhaustion and mourning, in an attempt to ease how much pain I was in and gain any relief from it at all.

When I met Logan and we just *clicked*, I'd stopped focusing on building anything more with other friends because he was surely The One. It's a lot like betting everything you have on that one slot machine, and if you win that's a huge win, but if you don't win, you just lost everything. And maybe it's better to bet on a few machines but leave most of your money in your pockets, in savings, in your own self-worth and self-esteem, which I didn't yet know how to do.

If you make one person your everything, you're more likely to do anything to make it work: ignoring things you're not getting, things you really should be talking about, just to make sure you don't lose it all.

On top of that, by putting all your resources and energy and time into one person, your other friends not only lose that time with you, but they aren't looped in anymore to tell you, "Hey, this friendship with Logan sounds a bit toxic, since you're both in love, or at the very least, you're now very much in love with him and waiting for a time when you can be together. I'd assess this a bit, I think!" We talk about abusers isolating you from your friends and family to gain more control over you and your decision making, and I don't want to brag, but I can do that all by myself!

In the most ideal of situations, we'd be able to be in a place with ourselves where we're enough as we are, and anyone can come or go, and we'll be OK. But when we're not in that place yet, because it's such a healthy, healed place that can be hard to get to, and take years or lifetimes to achieve, someone coming or going can shift our entire mindset. The loss can feel catastrophic. Because we're now relying on other people to feel good, to feel connected, to feel included, to feel safe, to feel worthy. And if they're gone, even if they still care about us, somewhere out there, we can feel completely unmoored, without a way to get back on land.

Where do you go now? You just start over? It takes so long to form deep, true bonds. But as hard as it is to realize this, you can't stay with someone just because you've put in this much time with them already. This "sunken cost fallacy" is something I've realized applies so much to friendships and relationships of all kinds: the idea that you've already sunk so much time into them you have to stay in them and keep working on it, or you'll lose what you "invested." But the truth is that when you put more time into something that isn't working, you're not getting that time back at all, you're just losing more of it. I think we often cling to this solution because it feels less scary and time consuming than trying to find a new person or having the patience to wait for that new person to come along.

Either way, if you're in love with your friend and you know you need more boundaries, the most important thing you can do is be honest with yourself, and with the other person, and set boundaries for yourself around it.

For me, it was great that I spoke openly about the will they/won't they happening in my friendship with Logan. And it was great that he acknowledged it, but I wish I'd set bigger, better boundaries around it instead of thinking I should probably set them and then allowing myself to be swept away by *Oh my god, he admitted it, he totally loves me!* while I silently remained his hypothetical girlfriend, waiting around for whenever he was emotionally ready to turn it from a hypothetical love to a real one that existed openly in the world.

And let me tell you, setting new boundaries with someone you're in love with and still want to be friends with can be extremely challenging and painful, which is why you might have to take a break until you're able to recalibrate and actually interact as just friends. And maybe in that break you'll realize you were never "just friends," and it only worked when you operated at a "wow there's tension here, and we're slightly dating without being open about it, in a way that doesn't always feel good for me, but oh well" level. Whatever the case, setting boundaries is like hitting a reset button on whatever you were doing before, so you can hopefully keep the love you shared and release the painful parts of things left unsaid. Your friendship might look a little different than before, and that's a good thing if what you had before wasn't working.

If you're meant to be together, finally having a friendship full of healthy boundaries will only help any romantic relationship you may have in the future. And in the meantime, let the "what ifs" go, and bet all your chips on yourself.

How to Adjust Your Friendship Levels: From Casual Friends to Close Friends and Back Again

Michael: What's going on, Rogelio?
Rogelio: I miss you, I mean we were in a pretty serious bromance. —*Jane the Virgin*

I have always had very good Stranger Luck, which is what I call meeting a total stranger briefly and really connecting with them for that moment in time in a way you weren't expecting. A good example of this happened a few years ago, when I was on an airplane and noticed a woman in a beautiful green coat in the row behind me. After we landed, there was a horrible snowstorm that made everything hectic, transportation-wise. I immediately called a cab to be ready for when we got off the plane, thinking there would be a war to find one. The nice coat lady behind me (she would later tell me) heard me make that call and thought, *Wow, that person knows what she's doing. I'm gonna follow her!* and waited with me at baggage claim before striking up a conversation. Several conversations about our shared love of Logan Echolls from *Veronica Mars* later, the two of us split a cab to Brooklyn. She was visiting NYC, and we hung out the whole time she was here, and we've been friends ever since. We don't talk all the time, or see each other all the time, but I love that a chance meeting developed into something more.

There is something so valuable and beautiful about friends I briefly made on the plane or subway or walking in the park. And they don't always have to transition into close friends! Having someone you connected with briefly in a really meaningful way is still a form of friendship, one with great value in its own right, even if you feel like it should become more than that for it to "count."

I've often struggled to be satisfied with connecting deeply with someone in passing and it not becoming a very close friendship you keep forever, at least partly because of how much we're socialized to value how long we've known someone over how much we've actually connected with them. In many of my experiences with Stranger Luck, those people might not have been a good fit for a deeper friendship but we worked so beautifully as acquaintances, or people who met for that one moment in time.

The truth is, having great Stranger Luck, and really memorable interactions like this is meaningful if it means something to you. Some of my favorite memories involve people I've only talked to for ten minutes, or met for one day. Those little moments when you connect with a stranger, for five minutes or five hours, meant so much to me, even if we never spoke again. And perhaps those relationships, as fleeting as they were, were meant to be exactly that. There are so many examples of friendships like this, that served their purpose at that time, and maybe aren't meant to be lifelong, and that's OK.

There's a group of women I met last summer when I was on tour and I was hanging out at the hotel pool alone before my show. One of them offered to take hot pool photos of me, and I nervously and then gladly accepted. They bought me one of the fancy drinks they all had, and we hung out in the pool for hours talking about everything, just everything, in that "girls you meet in the bar bathroom at two A.M." way that feels like a drug. And now we all like each other's social media posts devoutly, and every time I see them in my feed, I remember the very cool way we met. I didn't try to turn it into very close friendships, though maybe one day it will end up that way. But we should be able to see these friendships as beautiful just as they are, just for that moment in time.

Similarly, it would be great if all your friends from high school and college, or from your old jobs, were still compatible with you throughout the rest of your life, but for many of us, that isn't the case. And you don't have to keep them in your life forever, or try to remain just as close as you were, if that doesn't make sense to you anymore.

There can be friends you catch up with sometimes, or you reconnect with one day and it feels great, even if you don't become best friends again. Think of them as second-tier friends, which can sound harsh, but think of it less as "second-tier, wow an insult" and more like the second line of a friend-ship army. Maybe not someone you call when you're in an emergency, but someone you call to have fun. And over time and many life changes, maybe those friendships don't need to be kept up with as much, or someone wants more and you don't feel the same, or you get to a point when you realize you only want a few close friends, period.

Maybe things that worked for you years ago just do not work for you now. Maybe in high school, you loved having friends who gossiped and now you think that's really boring and not your thing. Or in your early twenties, you used to love friends who hated everyone, and now you want to be around people who love people more than they love to hate people.

Just as much as you're going to grow and change, it makes sense that your wants and expectations of your friendships will grow and change as well. So, if you used to love having thirty casual friends and now you want three very close friends because you just don't have the energy for anything else, that is great.

I know we love to think there's a magic number of friends you should have or maintain all the time, but not everyone has their set best friend or set friend group, and even if they do, they still might continuously shift. The social pressure of having a certain amount of, or type of friends is very much there, but that's just an external pressure that only gets really bad when you start to internalize it, when you start to believe it yourself.

The truth is if you have even one person in this world who feels like a good friend to you, you've won. But it's still so easy for that doubt to creep in, that fear that tells you you'll only be complete once you have whatever idea of friendship perfection you have in mind. And then on other days, you're completely fine with the friends you currently have, and your concerns lie more with figuring out how close friends you want to be, and where this friendship is headed. Not in a bridezilla way where you're looking for them to put a platonic ring on it, but when you have that interest in a casual friend, or a new friend, and you want to bravely explore what might be there, there are several directions this could go:

1. Casual Friends/Acquaintances
2. Friends
3. The Friend Group
4. Best Friend

The way many people navigate these is they have an acquaintance who they have a "spark" with, and they hang out with them casually until they start to wonder if that person is feeling as excited about this budding friendship as they are, and then they might want to have The Talk. But we'll get to The Talk in a minute. First, we must rant about how frustrating and overwhelming leveling up your friendships can feel.

How do you know who to let into your inner circle? How do you know how to do it? What words do you use? I can't tell you how many times I've had that spark with an acquaintance or friend and tried to level them up, only to realize that we're not compatible beyond that initial spark, or that we're much better as casual friends.

This is a nightmare, because sometimes that other person wants to stay Very Close Friends, and now you have to awkwardly put some distance between the two of you in a way where they don't feel rejected and you can just go back to Casual Friends, without anyone's feelings getting hurt. And hopefully without feeling any frustration at the situation yourself because damn it, it would've been so great if that could have been more, but sadly it cannot. No one's at fault, but now you're in this weird middle place, trying to figure out how to pull back without expressly writing a formal decree like:

Dear (person),

Thanks so much for auditioning to be my Friend. I really think you're better suited to the role of Casual Friend, which means we shall now cease all consistent communications and, instead, see each other at our mutual friend's birthday party once a year, at which time we will have a lovely twenty to thirty minute conversation and then occasionally like each other's social media posts.

Very cordially,

Your now Casual Friend

P.S.—This has already taken effect. Please do not text me about it, it will just be awkward for us both. Seriously, I don't hate you, I'm not mad at you, it is what it is.

God I would love to stop writing this letter now, it feels mortifying for us both.

This letter seems really appealing if you, like me, don't like the alternative, which is usually The Sudden Drift. This is when you realize you're better off as casual friends and don't want to talk about it, so now you have to purposely make your replies a little shorter, your response times a little longer, give increasingly less, until they hopefully get the hint. It's like soft ghosting someone you were once, even fleetingly, so close to, which can be interpreted as flakiness or rejection. So I never really want to do that, and it feels awful to have to.

Because of this process of having to "level back down" friends, I've often refrained from leveling anyone up at all; the risk of that rejection on either end leaves me feeling like it's not worth it to even try. However, my friend once told me she doesn't see it as a big deal, really. The way she sees it, people in your life can and will move backward and forward through those roles, and it'll all take care of itself. It's never personal, and she's right.

If anyone gets their feelings hurt in this process, they can always ask what's going on. But if you're like me, good lord you don't want to ask that! You don't want to say, "Hi, I feel like I've been downgraded, can you confirm or deny this? And if I have been moved, is there anything I can do to improve my relational dynamic with you because I really miss what we were?" particularly if you were close for a really long time, and this new dynamic doesn't feel as good to you.

It's another dating parallel: If you're friends with someone for a few casual months and you drift apart, it's safe to say it's not you, it's them. You're just not a good fit, oh well, find someone who is! But if you've had a longer, deeper connection, and that friend suddenly pulls away, it's completely fair to feel hurt by that and ask about it, whether they have the self-awareness or forthrightness to tell you what actually happened. And really, in both cases, it's not you, it's them. But that doesn't make the pain any less.

So if you're ready to move between these categories, one or both of you has to take that chance. Here's how you level up friendships:

1. **Share a little more about yourself with each other.** This can be as personal as you want it to be, but often the things that bring us closer are shared experiences, shared dreams, shared goals, shared fears. And you can only know you share those things by, well, sharing them with each other.

2. **Invite them to group outings and have them meet your other friends, thereby bringing each other into your worlds a little more.** If this seems overwhelming to you, don't worry, more on that later.

3. **Just keep getting to know them, in whatever way feels comfortable for you both, and whatever the friendship is meant to be will start to crystallize.** Once it does, you'll

either know exactly "what you are" or you'll feel the need to have The Talk.

The Talk

First of all, yes, the idea of having a formal relationship talk with a friend sounds ridiculous. But sometimes you really do need to know if they're as close to you as you are to them, even if it seems cooler to "not label it." How many times have you told a romantic interest that you didn't care if you labeled things, when you actually kind of did care? My guess is too many. Similarly, our friendships matter, and what we call them matters, and the process of wading through those uncertainties and how challenging it can be for many of us matters. Because we care, because we want community, because we are human.

I'm a huge "caring is cool" person. What if you acknowledged that yes, you want a close friendship, you want a Platonic Soulmate? And what if that repelled people, sure, but only the wrong people? And attracted other people who absolutely wanted that kind of deep friendship as well but thought it wasn't cool to say? And you got to be the brave one who said it, a relief for you both, that made it okay for them to say it too?

It's very human to want to make sure you're not too invested, or caring too much, or feeling like this is more valuable to you than it is to them. And if you're feeling that, it's really important to get clarity so you can stop constantly worrying if they *like you* like you (but as friends).

The way to do that is personal to you, of course, but if you need help with broaching this really tricky subject, here is how I—someone who hates talking about this stuff and knows the feeling of death by a thousand cuts that this kind of vulnerability can resemble—do it.

In a perfect scenario, it's clear that both of you want to level this friendship up because you're both reciprocating and driving the friendship forward. But if that's not the case, because of your respective insecurities or being socially awkward, here's what I'd advise.

You can start off by saying something, like, "I know you probably have a ton of close friends already, obviously, you're great. This friendship is really wonderful and important to me, and I'd love for us to be closer, if you'd like to. How do you feel about it?"

This acknowledges that yes, everyone has friends, and you're not trying to make it sound like you jumped off an alien spaceship and this is the only friend you've ever met, but this friendship really means something to you. You want to acknowledge how special that is to you, and maybe to them. The right friends for you will hear that and think, "Oh my goodness, I was thinking the same exact thing! This is really awesome, and we're becoming so close and it's so great!" The wrong people will not be on the same page as you or will have more neutral feelings about it. And at that point, it's up to you what to do with that information.

Good friendships are about two people mutually getting what they need from each other and being able to communicate openly to get to that point together.

This means that someone might see your relationship as a more casual friendship but you want something more, and it's at this point that you need to ask yourself if you'd really be comfortable being casual friends with someone you really want to be close to. Just in the same way that sometimes you don't always want to be just friends with someone you're falling in love with. Taking a look at how you truly feel about this, without judgment, is so important. If you're not willing to accept the depth of friendship they're offering, and you keep hoping they'll change, you might be setting yourself up for heartbreak.

There are definitely people I don't want to be casual friends with after they've been my go-to best friend for years. I don't want to have that shift; it feels too sad. But sometimes I've stayed in it just the same, hoping it will shift back. Many times, it has, and it was worth waiting, despite the periods of my feeling awkward and a little forgotten, and keeping the faith that we would be closer again once the timing was right.

Having that talk will, at the very least, clear up how they're feeling about you, so you don't have to wonder or guess or be nervous about it. It clears the air for you to know a bit more about how to proceed in this situation.

But how do you know if you've properly assessed this friendship (and now I sound like an insurance adjuster)? Here's how to tell if you're comfortable with your friendship level:

1. How does this friendship feel to you?
2. Do you feel like you're getting what you need out of this friendship, or are you always wanting more?
3. Do you often feel like you're giving more/less than they are?
4. Do you feel like you initiate plans more/less often than they do?
5. Do you often wish you were closer/less close than they seem to want to be?
6. Does something about your dynamic often feel strange and you can't put your finger on why?

If any of these are happening in a way that makes you feel uncomfortable and really bothers you, that might be a great sign that you need to level your friendship up or down.

Leveling down can feel like a breakup, and sometimes it is that simple, but sometimes it's just a shifting of expectations—seeing it less as "I thought this person would be there for me like a close friend, but it's just casual to them" and more as "This person is capable of less than what I need, but there are ways they *can* show up for me. Because these are the ways they can show up for me, I'm going to adjust my expectations of what kind of friendship we have."

It's really a gift you give yourself and, consequently, the other person as well. To be able to alter a dynamic so neither you nor they are constantly feeling disappointed or disappointing is a huge relief. To be able to see clearly that life changes, we change, and sometimes people can be closer to us, or not as close, and to honor those feelings while also still asking for what we truly need is really the best thing you can do for your friendships.

I've stayed in so many friendships, hell, I'm in a few right now, where we used to be closer, but they hurt me and we're not as close now. Or I pulled away because I wasn't getting what I needed and I didn't know how to ask for it, and they hadn't gotten my "I don't know how to ask for this directly" hints. Or they'd pulled away and I've asked them why, told them I missed them, but they remained distant, and it hurt to hear them tell me nothing had changed and they're just going through something. Because even if I believe them and know they're being honest with me, it's still painful to feel like I'm on hold. Did they hang up? There's no hold music at all?! Should I just be patient because they haven't technically hung up yet? Brutal.

And sometimes you really do just want to hang up, because your friendship might have too much damage to hold out for an answer.

But what if they eventually pick up? What if the friendship comes back, just as you remember it? It's a gamble. And the stress of the waiting period is often just not worth it if thinking about it causes you any kind of regular pain. Especially because while I stand by this being a rock-solid comparison, often people won't even admit they've put you on hold or have changed in any way. And in this case, there are usually one of two truths to grapple with:

1. **It really is just them, and it's not forever.** Sometimes someone really isn't in a place to be what they used to be to you. And it could be as simple as being busier than usual or going through a major life change, like getting married, or having kids, or moving, or going through illness or trauma, anything like that. And in this case, you just have to hope that one day you'll be able to have your friend back the way you had them before. And manage your own feelings about that (hopefully temporary) loss. But if you suspect it's deeper than that, then it might be this second answer.

2. **They don't want to continue this relationship with you, and they don't know how to, or don't want to, tell you that.** This one is so tough, because it's hard to know if this is the reason they're acting like this, since the whole point is that they won't clearly tell you. And as much as I would love to reach through this book and listen to your personal story about your friend who's acting weird lately and tell you for sure what they're thinking, I can't read their mind. And neither can you.

So if you can't bear waiting on hold while your friend navigates whatever is going on with them, or wait to find out whether or not it really is "just a weird time," or if they're ending things with you in a passive way, you really only have one option: To move on, as best you can.

If that means muting them, or even unfollowing them, because it's that painful, because just observing their lives in a parasocial way when they used to be close to you feels like a snake ate your stomach in one bite, do it. If you've already communicated what you need, and they're not able to give it to you, and so you need to set temporary boundaries online, but you're worried it might make things worse, or hurt them, it can be as simple as sending something like, "Hey, I have to do the following things right now while I'm processing this, but I'm still here, and you can reach out any time."

The whole point here is you have to do what's right for you. Just as they are doing what is right for them. Everyone's allowed to change and grow, absolutely. In the same vein, you're allowed to say, or simply feel, "What you can give me is less than what I need from you right now, so let's change how we interact, and here's how I need to do that in a way that feels right to me."

Being a good friend doesn't mean simply going along for the ride while the other person guides the friendship wherever they want to take it. You are allowed to say that you'd like this person to be X type of friend, and if they see it differently, they are allowed to say so as well. And then it is absolutely within your rights, and theirs, to either be OK with that difference or to part ways, no harm, no foul.

The most important thing to remember is that you were not made to endure your friendships. You were made to enjoy them. Adjust the levels as necessary.

Staying Friends with Exes: An Essential Guide

Men don't talk to people they've dated unless they want sex, or they're Winston. —Nick Miller, *New Girl*

I always marvel at people who say they're friends with all their exes. All of them? What on earth does that even mean?

I understand it in a way, as I have a rich history of being friends with people who I've always been kind of into, or they've always been into me, or we almost dated but I wasn't ready, so now we're just friends who have maybe frenched several times. That I get.

How do you remain friends with exes? Which exes do you remain friends with? When do you transition from partners/hookups/people who have frenched to friends? And should it take months, years, or tons of therapy and a dramatic mutual blocking of each other on social media before it can happen? How do you get through all the stickiness of whatever way it ended and your feelings about it?

It is almost always going to be complicated for at least one person, if not both, to navigate the mountain of feelings related to being friends with people you have "history" with, so when is it worth it, and when is it not?

I ask myself these questions every time I try to be friends with someone I found myself in that murky territory with, even if it was just "we almost dated but didn't," because for some reason, there is a chaos that is created when that threshold is crossed even a little bit. Some people can navigate this easily, and good for y'all! But even the people who are the best at navigating this are bound to have at least one partner who they want to stay friends with, who is seriously struggling with that concept on their end.

Many times, the person who has the hardest time transitioning is the one who definitely still has feelings, or both of you still have feelings but for whatever reason have chosen to just remain friends and lock those feelings in a chest in your attic that neither of you ever talks about but you both definitely have a key to it. It's there, on the key ring, occasionally taunting you and reminding you that "maybe it'll work this time!" But no, you shant use The Key, you mustn't. Oh no, I've made this scenario even hotter, my apologies.

Often these situations don't even begin with you actually being exes. So many friendships step into this territory as soon as attraction enters into the picture, whether you're both on the same page or not.

I have one such friend named Elyse who I met doing her podcast and right after we recorded the episode, she emailed me, extremely sweetly, and asked if I'd ever want to go on a date some time. I definitely did . . . aaaaand then went through a bunch of trauma and the timing just wasn't right.

We started going on friend dates and it was so wonderful. Elyse would send a car to pick me up, no destination given to me personally, and I would be whisked away to a cute Color Me Mine–type place to make mugs with her. She'd always pick up my favorite latte and bring it by when she came over. She just made me feel so loved and taken care of, the way a best friend would. I knew there were romantic feelings tangled up in it, but it also gave me the security of knowing someone was already "in" whenever I was ready to also be in. Still, she came into my life very clearly as a romantic interest. Friendship was there, yes, but I also didn't have to wade through the "should we be more?" or the "does she *like me* like me?" of it all either, which was, in some ways, the best of both worlds. Sure, I had to decide if I wanted to date her or not, but in that instance the ball was fully in my court, so the threshold for rejection was nearly zero, exactly as people with anxiety like it.

I didn't end up dating her at that time. I thought I might want to, might be able to, but I opted to set very clear friendship-only boundaries while I was still navigating the stickiness of the timing. I could've started to date someone while I was in a crisis, but I knew I wasn't in the best place to make decisions while I was in survival mode, and more than anything, I knew I really needed a friend in a huge way. And while yes, it could've been super dreamy and romantic to have a love interest swoop in to save me, the situation seemed ripe for codependency and me "needing" her to take care of me, and it seemed way too hard to find equal, healthy footing when I needed a nurse and a therapist way more than I needed a partner.

After months of a truly romantic and wonderful friendship, full of sweet moments such as Elyse buying a bunch of copies of my first book to give to people who couldn't afford them, getting me deeply thoughtful presents, and even helping me move, Elyse met someone she started dating. I was happy for her, until I began to feel sad. I don't know what happened, but one day when we were in a coffee shop, all of my "maybe, I don't know" feelings finally crystallized into "Uh-oh, I think I like you?" feelings . . . just as soon as she informed me she'd met someone. I laughed at first—*of course* this is when I got feelings clarity. But maybe they would be fleeting, and her new love interest would give me time to see if my feelings for her increased or if she was just unattainable now and looked extremely good that day in a cable knit sweater.

So, I let it go.

Elyse quickly fell in love with this woman who lived across the country, and they moved in together in a big house in the city. Elyse was now not only in love, which changed the dynamic of our friendship (it had to, of course, it had to), but now she was also moving away. Two gut punches. *I had my chance and I didn't take it.* I repeated that refrain in my mind for months after this, chastising myself for seemingly only wanting her as soon as I couldn't have her. Surely, I'd messed up and Elyse was my soulmate and now she was definitely going to marry someone else, and I was going to die of yearning within the next twenty-four hours.

The kind of yearning I had for Elyse wasn't often for Elyse specifically but rather a cute form of self-flagellation in which I would tell myself that she was my soulmate and I blew it. She became my source of comparison for every romantic relationship I had: "Elyse never would've treated me this way." She also became my source of comparison for every platonic friendship I had: "Elyse never would've treated me this way."

Both are probably unfair comparisons because she was never really just my friend or just my girlfriend but a blurred definition of both. In some ways, I think for most of my life that was exactly what I wanted from both my romantic and platonic relationships. But I clung to Elyse, as evidence that what I wanted in either partnership definitely existed, I'd seen glimpses of it, and I'd messed it up. Because I felt so conflicted about this, remaining friends with Elyse was like remaining friends with an ex: There were unresolved feelings, unfulfilled promises, and things left unsaid (by me) for the greater good of us both. Even though I knew, deep down, she was not my ex, I had to find a way to let go of these misplaced feelings; that wasn't as much the loss of a person as it was the loss of that type of deeply devoted kinship.

In a more clear-cut "staying friends with an ex" sense, I have quite a few. If it were up to me, I would stay friends with anyone I've ever meant something to, or who has meant something to me.

I think so many of us want the "let's stay friends" ending because we do not want to grieve any more than we already have. If you stay friends with your ex, it feels like the door is still open, for better or worse. On one hand, the door is still open for you to get back together one day, but on the other hand, the door is also open for a very murky friendship that is loaded with good and bad memories from the past, and untold possibilities in the future. Always in limbo, always kind of wondering. Especially when that person still feels like, or once felt like, the person you will end up with one day once you figure your shit out . . . or when they do.

A great example of this is Nick and Jess from *New Girl*, a show I have seen every episode of approximately 876 times. (If you've never seen the show and need to go watch it so you can experience the complex magic of Nick and Jess, go ahead, and then come back to this chapter.)

Nick and Jess are first introduced as a classic "will they/ won't they" pairing. Nick is a pessimist who had a rough childhood due to a real mixed bag of a great mom who relied on him a bit too much and a con artist grifter father who came and went from their lives, leaving his family with very little stability. Jess is an eternal optimist who had a great childhood, despite her parents' divorce and what seemed like pretty normal "I didn't fit in" experiences. Naturally, at first they clash constantly, resulting in increasingly heated disagreements that lead to, you guessed it, sexy, sexy chemistry.

The chemistry builds over season one, bringing them together in season two when they finally take the leap and get together. They're mostly great together, but they have some fundamental issues with how they want their futures to look, leading to their eventual breakup in season three. But of course, because Nick and Jess are seen as Meant To Be, and we believe this to be true, and the yearning is still present, albeit respectful (the hottest combination), we know this is not the end of their story.

We see Nick and Jess navigate the rocky initial breakup moments (see: the extremely sweet moment when Nick refills Jess's tissues for her while she's crying in her room of their shared apartment) and their occasionally still being into each other for a while, until it looks like they're moving past it, finally. Of course, as soon as Nick really starts to mature and enters into a serious relationship with Raegan, it is probably no coincidence that that's when Jess realizes she still has feelings for him, so much so that she can't be around him anymore. Their friendship has become untenable, despite how much it means to her. And at the very least, she can't live with someone she is still in love with, despite wanting to root for him, like a good friend would do.

And in true rom-com fashion, Nick increasingly realizes he and Raegan aren't great together largely because she just isn't Jess, and they break up. He realizes, through the help of his best friend Schmidt, that the real reason they didn't work is because he still is, always was, and always will be in love with Jess. After the appropriate amount of hijinks, they reunite, and we know this time it's forever because we're optimists and, well, we only have so many episodes left in the series.

That allure of "someday, maybe" is one of the biggest barriers I've found to remaining friends with exes because who's to say when it's really over? Is it really over, never going to happen ever, and you're just going to be close friends who tried and it didn't work once one of you is married? Maybe, maybe not.

The alternative seems to be only that the feelings you shared have been so obliterated by their (or your) actions, or your incompatibility that you would never ever go back to that relationship, ever. In which case, why would you want to be friends with someone who hurt you, or who is so much different than you are that you had to leave? Sure, you can be "friends" in the way that for a few months or even a year after the breakup you still text, hoping to make that smooth landing into genuine friendship, but this almost always fades out. Eventually, one of you starts dating someone else, or one or both of you realize you need space to grieve or separate. And then you'll become the kinds of friends who might still interact online, or still see each other around, but you've moved on, unable to turn the burner down on a relationship you had on high heat to the light simmer of a friendship without compromising everything that worked to begin with. The recipe is different, and it might not be as good.

The truth is, many exes will tell you they still want to be friends because they want to keep knowing you, because you mean something to them. But I have also known people who did not treat me well and wanted to "stay friends" so they could tell people, particularly future partners, "I'm still friends with all my exes" and maintain the image of being a kind and trustworthy person. A wolf in "I'm still friends with all my exes" clothing.

The key to being friends with your exes is, without a single doubt in my mind: very clear boundaries and communication on both sides.

It'd be nice to wing it, yeah, but you can't assume you both know how the other is grieving, what the other is expecting, or what the other needs during this sticky, complex process. And what will your new friendship look like? Is flirting allowed? Is bringing up other people allowed? And if so, when? Most of us don't want to talk about any of this, especially when we're still hurting, and in many cases, still hoping.

We've all been told that truly romantic moments happen when no one has to communicate what they want, what they're secretly hoping for, you just wait and pine and one day your ex will suddenly dump their lackluster partner and swoop you up in their arms, and you'll kiss, and you'll marry, and your friendship was all part of the grand love story you two were always destined to have.

And if it's not that, if your relationship was a life lesson, a period of mutual growth and love, but just not meant for forever, then what does the transition look like? Who are you now that you're just friends? How close are you? And *how* are you close? Do you become close in a way that your new partners feel threatened by, worrying that they're just a pit stop on the grand romantic journey of you two getting back together? Because that wouldn't be fun for someone else, and it wouldn't be good for either of you.

Nick and Jess worked best as friends when they were (mostly) able to let each other go, were (mostly) able to move on and be extremely into other people, even if there were still inklings that there was something there, that the porchlight was still on. But I think for it to be a truly healthy friendship, you have to dim that light as much as humanly possible and truly let any romantic expectation go. So, you know, I would not advise continuing to live across the hall from the ex you constantly turn to with each romantic upset.

Assuming your ex-turned-friend is your soulmate and one day you'll work it out and be back together can be harmful in so many ways that aren't always easily seen. In my experience, that belief often kept me from truly giving anyone else a shot. I would often think things like, "This person is nice, but we'll probably never have the connection I had with my ex," or "They'll probably never make me laugh the way my ex did," or that we'd probably never feel as meant-to-be as my ex and I did. And that belief turned into a deep truth, mostly because I continued to reinforce it.

There is no way someone you just met can compete with years of groundwork laid. These things take time, friendships take time, intimacy takes time. And one thing you have in spades when you've dated someone, and are now Just Friends, is hours logged. You have history. And compared to most new connections, a connection with someone from your past—even if it's imperfect and maybe even awful—feels far more comfortable.

The truth is, I don't think I'm someone who is able to be close friends with their exes. Every time I've tried to be friends with an ex in a real day-to-day consistent way there was always something off. I'm still friendly with some people who I dated briefly, usually because we were able to take a break after we dated, and then they met someone else, and I was happy to see them in the street, but we didn't talk with the same consistency, or the same level of intimacy that we used to.

If you're still in love with someone, or your ex is still in love with you, you both need distance before you can be friends. So give each other the space to move on, even though you'll miss them while they do.

While I can't tell you there's one right way to be friends with an ex, one way that always works, I highly recommend the following: Know what you need. Know what you want. Ask what they need. Ask what they want. Be as honest as you can. Because anything less is just another heartbreak waiting to happen. And we should strive to spare each other and, more importantly, ourselves, from heartbreak as often as we are able.

Friendships Are Relationships: Treating Friendships the Way We Treat Romantic Relationships

I found out what the secret to life is: Friends. Best friends.
— Ninny Threadgood, *Fried Green Tomatoes*

There seems to be this idea that friendships are easy, as though healthy friendships are just the accessories everyone comes with when they're born, and romantic relationships are harder and take work and communication and effort.

We never hear close friends say things like, "Yeah we've been best friends for six years. It's hard, sometimes! It definitely takes work, but it's worth it. You have to choose each other every day." That would sound so horrible, wouldn't it? You'd hear that and think, *Wow, you two guys should maybe stop being friends because that sounds COLD.* But when we hear someone who's been married a long time say it, we nod and smile and think, *Wow, they're really choosing each other. So sweet.* But I think we should start viewing friendships as relationships, because that statement is equally true for our friends.

It IS hard sometimes. It DOES take work, and hopefully, it is work worth doing.

If we started viewing friendships as relationships, we wouldn't feel like failures when we have to work on them, when we hit bumps in the road, when we both change individually and our relationship to each other changes as well. We would see it as a progression, as something we're both working on together, as two people who get to keep choosing each other, or not.

In romantic relationships, people tend to think that something is only a success if it lasts forever, and we have the same expectation with our friendships. If a friendship ends, we never say, "We just wanted different things." It can feel like once you're friends, you have to strap in and stay on the ride forever, or else you've failed. But I have friends who were my favorites and we're not friends anymore, and I will always hold them in my heart with neon lights around them. Do I wish they'd lasted longer? Yes! But if they didn't end in an emotional shoot-out in a saloon, I still hold them in my heart as a great success, because I think the most successful relationships aren't necessarily the ones that last the longest but the ones that made you the happiest.

So much of our conditioning, particularly for women, sets up for us to think that our job is to have a great family (super easy, everyone just gets that, sure!), find some great friends (again, easy! Just learn to socialize, have a little fun, don't think about it too much!), and then look for a partner. Your friends and family will be there while you look for romantic love, but don't worry, they're just the movie previews. The feature film is surely the person you will marry who will be everything to you and you will see your friends sometimes to complain about how he's "on your dick" about something. (That sounded more like a cliche of a husband, but I prefer to think of it this way here because it is more fun.) Then you go back home to him, your One True Love, your cup having been refilled with understanding and assurance from your friends. This is madness.

What if we put more weight behind *all* of our connections and allowed them to be richer, more conscious, healthy, and full? Think of how much freer we would be to make decisions about the types of people we have in our lives.

If you have a great friend group, you won't be in a rush to "settle" with the wrong romantic partner, because you've been able to develop that intimacy, that bond, that kind of love and companionship with your friends, so now you're not seeking one romantic partner to be the only community you have. And you have people in your life who are there to support you in this choice not to settle, even when society is screaming at you that you should.

I always wished we had more romantic comedies about friendships because these two types of love are so very similar. You meet someone in a cute way, you want it to be a little more, and then it becomes more, and more and more and more. And now you have a how we met story (I love a good friendship how we met story). You have history, you have a will they/won't they (become friends), you have all the makings of a great romantic comedy in which neither of you have frenched. Or you did once but have not since, etc., no judgment.

It can absolutely be just as hard to find a really great friend as it is to find a soulmate. And that beginning of a relationship when you're both playing a weird game of chicken to figure out if this has legs or if you're just trying each other on? Good god that exists in friendships. So let's explore things you might experience during the "What Are We" stage of friendship:

1. **Reading way too much into everything they say.** "Is this turning into a thing?" is something I say virtually every twenty minutes while reading texts from someone I have

a crush on *and* also a new friend I am really excited about. Are they just bored and I'm a fun new text friend, or are we also mutually mentally planning a friendship road trip for three to four months from now, or maybe next week because I'm around?

2. **Trying to figure out how to say goodbye in a casual way usually turns into you half-hugging them and running away.** Running away at the end of the first few friendship hangs with someone is one of my favorite pastimes/coping mechanisms. Mostly the latter.

3. **Being so nervous about making plans for the next time you see them that you just leave before it can happen.** Because what if I ask them what they're doing next weekend, and they say, "Um, I have my own life, next week is too soon and I saw this as more of an every three months friendship," but they're too polite to say it outright, and then I have to figure that out from their tone and body language cues. No, thank you, bye.

4. **Not wanting to assume that everyone who is passively nice to you wants to be real friends with you, so you assume no one ever wants to be real friends with you.** This has been my plan since I was thirteen and I've been happily unsure of my personal connections ever since (JK, this plan is terrible).

5. **The more you like someone, the more terrified and nervous you become.** My friends are always trying to tell me to "calm down" and "stop breathing into that paper bag every night when you think that this new friendship might actually be something cool because that means it could end and then where will you be," but I don't listen.

6. **You worry about making the first move.** Have I tried

asking a stranger who I felt I had a cool connection with if they wanted to be friends and then it turned into three fun texts and a mutual ghosting? Yes, I have. And because of this, the last time I made the first move was about four years ago and I don't plan to do it again!

7. **Someone you hit it off with says they want to hang out sometime and you debate in your head for two hours whether it's worth it.** I mean, they could be great or they could be mean or weird or I don't like them as much, or they don't like me as much, and then we're trying to make it work when it just doesn't . . . oh. They already walked away, like twenty minutes ago. Hm.

8. **Wanting to be Best Friends so badly that you start romanticizing that future possibility to an inappropriate degree.** Basically falling in love with the idea of how close you could be, cute things they could do, cute things you could do, to the point where you've now written this friendship rom-com in your head without them and you don't even know their middle name yet.

9. **Wanting to scream, "DO YOU WANT TO BE BEST FRIENDS?" during conversation but having to hold it in.** Once I full-blown like someone, it's all I can do to not shout this every twelve minutes.

10. **Being so terrified of first-friend-date silence that you end up telling a really personal and upsetting story.** Probably about your gut microbiome or how your parents died in a fire. Neither one goes super well with noodles. But to be fair, some of my favorite friendships started off with unintentional mutual trauma blurting that turned into laughter and a solid bond, so it could go either way.

There is just as much of a pressure to be chill in the beginning—if it happens, it happens. But for people who tend to be more introverted, or anxious, "just going with the flow" can feel awful and therefore could stop friendships before they even start.

Just like with romantic relationships, we bring our baggage with us to every single friendship we embark on, trying to size it up for how we might get hurt this time. If you don't do this, count your blessings because the possible disasters are many. But I think for most of us, even when we're feeling brave and hopeful, we want to know the ending. We want to know where this goes.

In some cases, we may even seek out reasons it would never work. They are extroverted, you're more introverted. They're a Gemini and you're someone who has seen a lot of Gemini slander in memes, and what if those memes are right? It's easy to look for the red flags in the beginning stages because you're not as invested yet, and most of us want to keep ourselves from getting too invested in something that might not work out, to spare ourselves possible pain.

And even if you are reaching for reasons it wouldn't work, some of those reasons might have some truth to them, especially if one of you is more extroverted than the other, or vice versa. That can be a very real and valid difference. If you're a planner and they text you the day of, "I'll let you know what my plans are in a few hours!" you might see that and think, "Oh, you mean at eight P.M. when it is currently five P.M., and by eight P.M., god knows where my head will be at, but it will likely be on a pillow on the couch while *How Stella Got Her Groove Back* plays in the background? Yeah, good luck there."

It can be wonderful to have friends who are more spontaneous than you are, but if you're someone who feels social occasionally and then needs days to recover and curl up inside a little pile of blankets, they might not understand that. To them, you haven't hung out in weeks, but in your mind that's because they keep inviting you to get wasted in a warehouse, when what you might want most lately is a cup of coffee and to just talk with them.

People who only have so much social energy in them are rightly picky and protective of it. If I spent my reserves of social energy on a party I hated every second of, it can fully consume my brain for days, in a way that someone whose extroversion refills every two seconds may not understand.

You might need to know how your night will go so you can know if it sounds worth it, not because you're a king and you need to know if it's worthy of your presence, but also now that I think of it, that's totally it. Similarly, if you're already out with friends and someone says, "We're going to a really cool bar after this. You should come with us!" And you want to glare at them like, "Sir, have you ever tried to get an extroverted introvert (a very introverted person who seems outgoing but mostly wants to stay home, which some people would argue is just a person and I will not debate that because I would rather stay home) to a second location in the same night?" That makes sense to me! Or you had plans to meet up with a friend and on your way to see them they said, "My friends Dave and Penelope from work are coming too, hope that's OK!" which sends you into a panic spiral because this was not the plan? Makes sense too!

It can be really hard to maintain a friendship when you prefer small intimate gatherings and they like larger groups.

Sometimes when I say I'm feeling lonely, and someone suggests I come hang out with them and twenty other people at a club, I don't know how to say, "Oh, I meant I want one or two people to come over and preferably they would bring chips because I do not have chips." This is really where it pays to either befriend only other introverts, or at least very understanding extroverts who won't ever make you feel bad for needing the alone time they rarely seem to need. And we don't want to be frustrated by these differences, but it makes sense that we might be, and then worry we could never truly be friends because of them.

It's so tempting to run through all these scenarios in our head, just like we would at the beginning of a romantic relationship. We ruminate on how things would probably never work anyway because they're more outgoing, or they're more antisocial, and all of the hypothetical reasons to cut and run. In both romantic relationships and friendships, it's natural to want the reassurance that "This Is It, this will last, this will be worth it, and this time we won't get hurt like we did before." But unfortunately, none of us are that psychic (yet, I'm working on it).

The best thing you can do is to be the best possible friend you can be, communicate and listen, and sit with those uncomfortable "how's this going to end?!" feelings as they arise. Just stay in the present moment as much as you can, and cross your fingers that you'll one day get to tell your "How We Met" friendship story, with all of the "I was so nervous!" parts behind you, ultimately leading your friendships to the places you always hoped they would go.

Being Friends with Coworkers, Roommates, and Family Members: How to Navigate Them All

Office administrator Pamela Beesly-Halpert is my best
friend. I'd say I have gotten along with my subordinates.
—Dwight Schrute, *The Office*

There are so many potential paths to friendship in our adult
lives: friends you grew up with or went to school with, work
friends, family members, neighbors, people you see at the
gym who you mostly ignore because you're focused on getting
through yoga in one piece. In every situation, there might be
people who would be a good fit for us, but the paths to culti-
vating that friendship aren't often well defined for us or, if they
are, seem totally impossible to achieve.

We see *Gilmore Girls* and assume we'll be best friends with
our kids or our parents. We see *New Girl* and assume we'll be
best friends with our roommates. We see *Parks and Recreation*
and assume we'll be best friends with our coworkers.

We romanticize and idealize this seemingly very easy
thing where we're best, best friends with the people in the
spaces where we often spend the most time: our workplaces
and our homes. And post-college, we're told that we're most
likely to meet our friends at work. Because where else would
you meet them? Yay, zero work-life balance!

But we never talk about how to navigate those friendships despite them having the great potential to have zero boundaries in the places we need them the most: work, family, and our home.

So, if we get along with people we share these spaces with, what types of friendships are possible there? What do they look like? And are they the same as our other friendships outside of those spaces?

While it would be great if all of these interactions were as idyllic as they are in the movies, they rarely are. So let's look at the pros and cons to each of these, and how to navigate them in a better way.

Pros and Cons of Being Friends with Your Roommates

There's a reason this is such a common TV trope, because you get to live with your friends, for better or worse. You get to have lazy brunches and dinners in your kitchen, and no one has to check their schedule because you know when they're around.

The other side of this is that sometimes you just want to be alone and pretend your roommates don't exist. Like if you woke up grumpy and don't wanna chat early in the morning and just wish to move around your home like a sleepy ghost for a while without them feeling hurt by it. And you might not always want them to join you in things you're doing, which can be tough to communicate. I once had a roommate come into my room when my date and I were watching a movie, and she, for real, got on my bed and WATCHED THE MOVIE WITH US. The whole time. For two hours. It was a nightmare. Should she have known better? Yes! And I still don't know why she did not. We are not currently close.

You might also find that having friends as roommates means you're less likely to have passive-aggressive "clean the dishes, don't just soak them!" notes everywhere, but sometimes your friends are actually more passive-aggressive than they would be with a stranger because having to remind your friend to do those things feels extra annoying. Hopefully you're living with a friend who is able to communicate clearly and respectfully, but it can be really hard to do that.

Still, there is something to be said for having the right people there when you really want someone to be there. For instance, it's absolutely marvelous to be able to ask your roommate if your outfit looks great before you go out. Cher in *Clueless* said that nothing beats taking Polaroids of your outfit, but she didn't live with a best friend who has great taste and is brutally honest when it comes to faux-fur jackets you bought for two dollars at a somewhat haunted thrift store. And when you get back from a date, there's no better feeling than walking in the front door and seeing your friends sitting in the living room waiting to hear all about it and you get to pretend you're in a romantic comedy. And if you bring your date home, you can get a second opinion on them without making a whole to-do about meeting the friends. To them, they're just coming to your apartment, and to you, your friends are silently judging whether or not they're good enough for you. Very subtle, very effective.

Having friends who live where you live means you always have someone to watch a movie with, or borrow clothes from, or if you run out of milk, they have milk. All of this is great, with one caveat, which is the fine line between "we use each other's stuff all the time anyway," and "welllll, I used to feel that way, and now I realize she mostly uses my stuff and I've essentially become a CVS for someone who is supposed to be my best friend and I don't want to bring it up because we both live here." This is especially true if you're not into mutual sharing and they really are, and you've told yourself to just be "chill" about it, but you finally realized you have never been and probably never will develop said chill.

Outside of the physical benefits of this, the emotional benefits of living with your friends are many, namely that you have someone to save you from yourself. All you've done for two days is watch *You've Got Mail* on a loop and eat nachos? They know, and they are intervening. Plus, you always have someone to worry about you if you don't come home. Ideally, nothing ever actually happens to you and you're always safe and sound, but for those nights when you crash at a friend/hookup's place, there's nothing sweeter than getting the "Hey, are you OK? You didn't come home last night and I'm worried" text. Even though you're totally fine, this text feels like a hug.

The biggest benefit of all is that *you live with your friend*! You don't have to think about who you should text when you're feeling bad because you have a close friend in the next room who can probably tell you're sad, or at the very least, you can knock on their door and give them a look that tells them you need every hug. It's a built-in support system.

And on the other side of this coin, living with your friends also means you're sharing financial responsibilities with your friend, which can be great if you're both the same kind of financially responsible, but if you're not, welcome to hell, aka "one of us becoming the person who has to make sure the other one actually pays their share of the bills because the other one forgets and now there's resentment and weirdness and someone keeping track of how much you still owe." A nightmare. And if you have a conflict or issue with that person, not only does this affect your friendship, it literally affects your living situation. So now you're stuck in that nightmare scenario of feeling weird in your own home because of some drama happening between the two of you, which is enough to make you justify selling your organs so you can finally live alone and never have to feel this way again.

It'd be great if living with your friends was always the way it was on TV, but the truth is often that the highs are high and the lows are low, which leads us to another scenario where that's very much the case: being friends with your coworkers.

Pros and Cons of Being Friends with Your Coworkers

Ah, the dream of being friends with your coworkers. This is such a complex thing, because if all goes well, you really do get the best working environment. You're excited to go to work because all your friends are there, so it really feels like having community at the place you're in most of your day.

Having friends at work truly feels like you're getting paid to hang out with people you love, and it is one of the greatest, rarest gifts. You can vent to them about your boss/coworkers because they already know that Derrick In Accounting seems to be a genuine haunted mystery of a person, and having this running joke is really priceless.

Plus, there are the practical rewards of your work friendships potentially resulting in you getting promoted, or getting a raise, because people really like you and want to work with you. If you're lucky enough to have that *Parks and Recreation* dream where you really love these people and they love you, you're able to be a united force that can make your workplace better for you all.

But while all the perks are undeniably there, being friends with your coworkers still might be very unachievable for some of us, which we rarely talk about. Your workplace may be really cliquey, or your coworkers are just very different from you, or you have a lot of social anxiety, partly because of the very real fear of what could happen if these friendships don't work out, or even if they do.

Not to mention, if you don't work in an office, or are in a more creative field, then you're tasked with "networking" by way of making friends in your industry. Since there's no one office where you'd meet them, it can be far more work to seek those people out, and navigate if they're just going to be networking connections, or friends, and feeling out what they want from the relationship as well. Are you making a new friend, or did they only say they want to be friends as a way to be polite? Either one is fine, but the stress of that can sometimes make you want to scream, "It's OK if you just see us as networking friends, but you don't need to tell me we're going to be best friends to get that." Because it can really hurt to get very excited about a new friendship with a colleague that they may see as something more transactional, despite what they're saying.

Granted, most people genuinely don't know what they're looking for yet, but sometimes you do meet someone in your field who says, "OK we're going to be friends" and you get excited and start acting like a friend and oops, they just meant "We will be people who network and get along, so why are you texting me on Friday night asking me what my favorite *Scream* movie is?" and it's disappointing. And then you have to reassess where you've placed them in your life. Or they said they want to be friends, really meant they wanted to be friends, but "friends" to you means more than the effort or energy they're currently giving you, and now you have to find a way to navigate that.

It's kind of like a job application. They applied for the job of Friend, or Best Friend, and there were qualifications for that job that you needed them to meet, and they are not meeting them. Similar to the formal decree, I wish you could send them a rejection letter for the job they weren't a good fit for. Something like:

Dear (person),

Thank you so much for your interest in being my friend. As of right now we are looking for certain qualities in the person who is going to fill this position, and it is not your particular skill set. You may, however, be a good fit for our networking friends position, which we encourage you to apply for. Either way, thank you so much for your interest in my company and I wish you the best of luck in your search.

Sincerely,

I hate having to write this.

But the awkwardness of this "what are we?" aspect is just the beginning of the potential pitfalls of becoming friends with your coworkers. For starters, it's so much easier to stay at a terrible job because all your friends are there. The bonds of a slogging through a bad job together are formidable, yes, but it's also very easy to stick it out in a place where none of you are happy or feeling good about what you do, just because you love one another and don't want to lose the friendship.

It can also be hard to know who to vent to, or what alliances exist that you don't know about. If you've ever started at a new job and vented to someone about your boss/coworker and then later noticed they're best friends with them and you're like "ohhh whoops" you know this feeling well. Similarly, if you have a falling out with a work friend, it could be hard to know who to trust or befriend in the office now, or feel like you can't befriend anyone else because the potential fallout is too stressful. If that work friendship falls apart, or you were never able to make those work friends for whatever reason, you might not have that support network, which could directly impact your ability to get promoted, or get brought onto other projects because now you're not in the "clique," maybe even through no fault of your own, and it feels awful.

I wish this wasn't true, and I hate it so much. We rarely talk about how much being able to "fit in" at work and have a group of tight-knit work friends gives you a leg up at work. And if you're misunderstood, or ostracized, or aren't sure how to navigate that, or just don't want to do it, it could have a direct financial impact on you, even though it shouldn't. People want to hire their friends, and they might not remember people they don't talk to or see as often, so then you're supposed to stay close with "the right people," but it's hard to know who those people are. What if you don't really click with them and aren't able to pretend you do, or don't see them as people you want to be that close with? It's exhausting to navigate. And it can be especially challenging if you later have to distance yourself from a coworker-turned-friend, or move them from close friend status to an acquaintance for your own peace of mind. And now you have to worry that you've put yourself in jeopardy at work, which is a position no one should ever have to be in. But ohhh, it happens.

Similarly, let's look at the idea of being best friends with your family members, which is arguably the dream, and often the most difficult one of all three of these to navigate.

Pros and Cons of Being Friends
with Your Family

For anyone who is already seeing this section and laugh-crying because even the idea of being friends with their family at this point is absurd, I will direct you to my first book, *How To Be Alone*, because we never talk about how painful and hard and impossible it can be to be close to your family in the ways you want to, or the ways you've been told you should be close to them, and I will always want to talk about that.

But for now, let's assume you're close with your family and that is something you're able to do to some degree, even if it's not always perfect. If that's you, here are some high points (which are mostly imagined by me and based largely on what I've seen on fictional television shows):

The pros of being friends with your family members are just so many, mainly because you hit the lottery: You were born to warm, loving people who are able to openly love you, see you, and relate to you. I feel drunk right now even writing about the idea of that. Not everyone gets this at all, and unfortunately, so many of us were born to people with their own generational trauma and a lack of tools to be the kinds of parents they wanted to be, and the kinds of parents you needed.

The ability to have your family actually be your friends means you have friends who've known you since birth, so they know all the same random movie quotes and that running joke that started when you were nine years old that's still funny when you bring it up now. They have a lifetime of shared memories. They've known all the people you were, the child that you were, the teenager you were, all of the pieces of you no one else saw. If you're lucky enough to have this, they're able to love you and see you in a way that is so special and so rare.

As much as it's amazing that you have a shared history, that also might mean you share some trauma and it might be easier for that old pain to come to the surface much more easily when you're around each other, even in the best circumstances.

So the cons here boil down to needing boundaries, far more than with our coworkers or roommates, because we're told that family is all that matters. We don't think of family as being a relationship that requires boundaries, but I would argue that families are where boundaries are most necessary—partly because it's so easy to become blindly loyal to your family, to defer to them, ignoring your own feelings because "blood is thicker than water," no matter what. But these relationships are absolutely a great place to form boundaries and check in to make sure everyone's actually feeling good and not just pretending for the sake of appearing like a "good family."

This often extends to any kind of fight with a family member, which could quickly turn into a situation where people can choose sides and a simple disagreement or a bid for more boundaries could quickly turn into a genuine nightmare of seismic proportions. Because it's not just a fight between you two now, it's a fight between you and your grandma and your other parent and your siblings and everyone has opinions and, good lord, you just wanted to set a few boundaries on a weekend!

There is so much in our culture that tells us to have blind allegiance to our families, no matter how they treat us, or if they violate our boundaries, or if they're abusive, and we have to stop reinforcing this as a truth. So the most important thing to remember in your friendships with your family members is that *your needs matter too.*

There is nothing shameful or antagonistic about asking for what you need, or having different needs than you used to, and asking your family members to meet them. Even if it sounds weird to them, even if they don't understand why you need them, even if you didn't need them before and they don't understand what changed. If someone loves you, truly loves you, they will make it a priority to give you the things that you need and ask for directly.

In all three instances, these cons can contribute to our fears and beliefs that finding friendships that feel healthy and good to us are impossible, because it's just not as simple as what we've been told. There's danger and joy within any of these situations, but there is also power in remembering that you have agency.

You have the ability to discern and assess and reassess every one of your relationships with your family, coworkers, roommates, you name it, and set any boundaries as you see fit. You can always adjust as necessary, and remember that even though these situations can feel powerless—*But they're my family! But we work together every day! But I live with them!*—you always have power in these situations.

You can absolutely change the way you engage, or stop talking to that family member, find a new job, or find a new apartment if any of these relationships has become harmful to you. And in each of those situations, what may seem like a devastating blow to life as you currently know it, may actually be a blessing; a necessary rerouting to a better path which will lead you to the people who *are* right for you. The people you get to choose.

How to Fight with Your Friends: When It's Healthy and When It's a Warning Sign

I am so fucking sick of all of you. —Shoshanna Shapiro, *Girls*

In most of the depictions of friendship I saw growing up, friends never fought. They would have, at most, one big fight in the whole series when you were thinking, *Oh no! What if they break up?!* but of course they never did. But even still, it was a huge deal to fight with your friends. It was explosive, it would happen once, and oftentimes it would show two friends really hashing out all their issues (we see this in *Yellowjackets*, *Jennifer's Body*, *Parks and Recreation*, *Romy and Michele's High School Reunion*, *Glow*, *Buffy*, *Insecure*, *Girls*, *Mean Girls*, hell, even *Practical Magic* when they're drunk on haunted ghost wine) and then they were (mostly) fine forever after that. Well, except for *Yellowjackets*, RIP Jackie. And *Jennifer's Body*. Wow, a lot of death in some of these . . . ANYWAY.

I know why people write fictional friendships this way. In my ideal friendship, we would rarely, if ever, fight. So as a viewer, it's exhausting and stressful to watch these characters you're rooting for in an uncomfortable situation where they're saying things they both mean and haven't communicated properly before, but are also saying a lot of things you know they don't mean, and the fight has become so heated that now they're just hurting each other because, well, fighting *hurts*. For many of us, fighting is exhausting and scary and can make us question if our friendship is in jeopardy.

Are you right? Are they right? Are you both right? And how do you move forward from this fight? How do you make it less of a "fight" and more of a conversation that's productive and helps guide you both to whatever happens next? Because maybe you WILL realize you're not meant to be friends and maybe you WILL be too hurt to continue. Those outcomes are possible. So is there a way to fight where you can at least attempt to minimize the unnecessary harm you cause each other and yourself? In my experience, there is.

Although people can be quick to say that couples who fight are healthy, and if you're a couple who never fights and never disagrees, there's something wrong, we're less likely to say that about friendships. There seems to be a belief with friendships that you'll never fight ever, and if you DO fight, something is definitely wrong, which is why so many of us, myself included, will keep years of frustrations about our friendships bottled up. And in some cases, we're doing this because we know that if we fully address the feelings we're keeping inside, we might realize this friendship isn't working for us anymore, and we may need to leave.

Then there's the other side of this coin, where you're fighting too much. "Too much" is of course relative, and I would say if you feel like you fight with your friend too much, you probably do. Because as always, you're allowed to define these boundaries, you're allowed to define what doesn't feel good to you, and if you've already made a good-faith effort to communicate that to your friend and you don't see any changes, then it's OK to make that call.

It's OK to say, "We fight too much. For me personally. Maybe someone else would be alright with the amount we fight, and maybe you're okay with the amount we fight, but I'm not."

Because we make it seem like fighting with your friends is such a bad thing, I've had very few fights with friends, and in retrospect I really wish I had been more confrontational. As a recovering people-pleaser, I was never ever going to start fights, no, no. I would whisper my needs and sulk when they were not met. Far healthier!

And I've come to realize that if we do that, we're never fighting, but we're never clearing anything up either. We're never allowing ourselves to fully be heard, and thereby allowing the other person to tell us why they feel or act the way they do.

For me, the fear is that they will admit the reason they acted a certain way is because they don't really care about our friendship, don't really care if they hurt me, and that they're doing it intentionally. But the truth is, more often than not, those things are just misunderstandings and miscalculations of what they thought you needed. But you can't know that until you "fight," in whatever way works for you.

It's absolutely possible to fight with a friend in a way where neither person is yelling. Especially if you, like me, hate yelling, or hearing yelling, and it just makes you want to cry. I never want to yell during fights, but hey, if both of you love to passionately shout your boundaries, I've done this before and I could see why people like it. There's yelling AT someone, which can seem like an attack, and then there's a "damn it, I've kept these needs inside me for so long that I need to shout them so I'm finally heard. I'm sick of being scared to voice these, I hope that's OK, here goes!" yelling that sometimes you need to do, especially if you're scared of it and it's new to you.

Fighting in a healthy way doesn't need to involve serious yelling at all and should allow you both to feel heard by each other, identify core needs, and address real concerns in your friendship. Steering away from blame and things like "you always do this"—the things people often tell couples to steer clear of when fighting—can go a long way in being able to address real concerns in a friendship.

If you can do this in a good-faith way, where you're saying what you need and how their behavior has felt to you, and they're able to do the same, it actually creates an opening for a deeper intimacy and understanding for each of you, which can make your friendship even stronger than it was. And yes, it still can hurt when you're fighting and they disagree, or they can't or won't see your perspective, which absolutely happens. The main goal here should be to see your fights as an opportunity to truly communicate and set boundaries, and, above all, gather information about the current health of this friendship.

If your friendship were a car and you never took it to a mechanic to see how it was running, you'd never really know what's going on with it, and eventually the car might just die because you never looked under the hood. Friendship is the same way. Yes, it can be scary to look and see what's going on in there, but if you can figure out a way to make it productive—no fault, no blame, just two people working together to find common ground—and it's done well, it can be an opportunity for you to both meet each other where you are, and grow and change together.

But sometimes there is fault, there is blame. Someone *did* do something hurtful, or there was a misstep, and you need to talk about it, which is admittedly harder to face, as it requires accountability on their end and the ability to forgive on yours. Or vice versa. It also might require you to see something from their perspective that will show you something about yourself that you may not like.

Healthy fighting should be productive, not punitive. We should be able to see it as something that's worth doing, so you're both able to talk out conflicts when they come up. And if you still can't reach an understanding, then at least now you know this might not be right for you anymore. And you can move on to better friendships, better connections, with a greater knowledge of what doesn't work for you and what you need. Leaving something that isn't working for you or doesn't feel right to you is a gift you're giving both of you. It's permission for you to seek something better for yourself, and permission for your friend to do the same.

Friend Breakups: How to Know When to Leave, How to Do It, and How to Cope with the Grief

Even though we meet as strangers now I still love her with an inextinguishable love.
　　　　　—Anne Shirley, *Anne of Green Gables*

As much as it can be heartbreaking if someone turns out to be not what they seemed, or for your friendship to not be the forever friendship you'd hoped it would be, the upside is that this can bring you to the realization that you can trust yourself. Your suspicions that these are not the right friends for you anymore and that there is nothing you can, or should, do to fix it are warranted. I've found myself in this exact position so many times, but it shifted in a larger way only in the last few years. It is so beyond frustrating to realize that your "I finally have friends, yes! I did it!" was a bit of a false positive, and actually some of these friends are still kind of bad, and you just want to shout "AGAIN? Seriously?" And when it happened this time, I realized a lot of my friendships were still being chosen from the places where I was not yet healed and therefore my friendships were still not working, even if progress had been made. Realizing that was what was happening freed me to take a step back and reevaluate what I was tolerating, and what wasn't mine to fix. I was, for the first time ever, allowing myself to say, "I tried my best in this friendship," let it go, and focus on people who did love me and did care. Was it easy? Oh goodness, no, it was not.

For most of my life, I thought that friends were whoever chose you, who ever applied for the job. But now I realize that *you deserve to choose who you let into your life.* You get to choose who has access to you. And as hard as it can be, sometimes you can only meet the right people once you release the wrong ones who aren't making you happy and change the rules for who gets access to you.

This can be so hard to do though, especially because when you love someone, you're invested, and you've put in the time to find a way to fit together. But everyone is a puzzle piece, and you can't always see why the edges don't quite line up when you're together, but you know it when they don't. You feel it.

You want to grow, you want to be better, but what if as you do, that you realize there are people who don't fit in your life anymore? Sometimes the people you bonded with in the past fit you well at the time because you were wounded in the same way. But the more you work on yourself, the more you heal, the more you grow, and they don't fit anymore, you will wonder what warped them. Was it weather? Did someone get this puzzle WET??? But the truth is *you* have changed shape. *Your* edges have softened, *you* have expanded. Maybe they stayed the same. Maybe they contracted or expanded in a different way. But you don't fit anymore.

On the surface, this is growth, this is the goal. But no one really tells you what growth can cost you. You want the people you came with to follow you to this new place. To grow as you grow, alongside you.

We believe that partners come and go, yes, but friends and family are forever, they are our constants. And I want my constants like they are free breadsticks at an Olive Garden. You told me I get them, I know other people got them, I saw them on TV, and I swear to god if you don't bring them out for me soon I will smash every window in this Cincinnati mall location!!!

We spend so much time in our childhoods learning about practicing fairness, but the world itself is not fair, as much as we'd like it to be. We're not all walking the same path, with the same resources and the exact same timing. Ideally, we'd all get the support systems we were promised, but then some of us don't, and no one taught us how to fill in those cracks. No one teaches us how to find power in vulnerability, how to build intimacy, how to grow as a person, or how to grieve when you've outgrown the people you once loved. Or when they outgrow you. And they definitely don't teach us how to navigate the anxiety that can come up in your friendships. I am so endlessly nervous around some of my friends, which I assume you're not supposed to be. But just the same I am often plagued with worry: What am I allowed to need? Who am I allowed to be? How much imperfection will people allow? And is having these anxieties about the friendship more about the baggage I have from my past, or is this friendship wounded, or worse, broken entirely?

So here are some signs your friendships are not working for you anymore. This doesn't mean they're irreparable, but you may need to talk things through. Again, recognizing these patterns is all about gathering information, so you can know what you need to do next:

1. **You can't remember the last time you felt good around them.** Your relationship to each other might change often, or every now and then, but if you no longer feel like you have fun together, or you're still getting too weighed down from past hurts, or you're hanging out with them out of a perceived obligation because you've known each other so long, that's a sign.

2. **You stress about the way you communicate with each other.** If something about this friendship causes you to feel anxious about how often, or how much they reply to your texts, and this stresses you out regularly and consistently, even though you've told them what you need, that's a sign.

3. **You don't feel supported by them.** Your friends shouldn't be passive in their support of you, or worse, visibly competitive with you, so if you often feel like when you ask for help, they're tepid and don't seem to care, even when you've communicated what you need them to say or do in that situation, that's a sign.

4. **Your other friends make you feel more loved than this friend does.** While it's hard to compare friendships, if you notice there are some friends who you always feel super loved and supported by, but you don't ever, or very rarely, feel that with this friend, ask yourself why that is. And if it's something that can be discussed, bring it up to them! But if it feels fundamental, that could be a sign it just might not work well. Some people are just a better fit for you than others. It's such a gift to have friends who make you feel the way you want to feel in a friendship, and often they make it easier to realize that maybe it's time to release the friends who don't.

5. **You're happy less than sixty percent of your time together.** This number is very generous, but if you're not happy with your friendship at least most of the time, that's a sign.

6. **You feel like they treat their other friends better than they treat you.** This one is so brutal when it happens to you, and yes, everyone has different levels of closeness with people. But if you notice they're able to give the things you've told them you need to other people but not to you, that's a sign.

7. **You've started to think maybe you can't have everything you want in a friendship.** If you've started thinking that maybe your dream friendship doesn't exist and perhaps this is the best you can do, seriously, that's a sign. Your friendships should feel like you won the lottery, not a consolation prize.

Sometimes the reasons for the friendship breakup really are just that you've realized you're no longer getting what you need from them, if you ever did in the first place. It might not even need to be toxic for you to decide to break up with them, it can just be that the friendship isn't making you happy anymore. That is so important to note. There have been so many times when I didn't want to end something because it wasn't completely toxic, but oftentimes, simply staying in a friendship that isn't working for you anymore, and some part of you knows it, can *become* toxic.

But even the more classically toxic friendships can still be hard to spot when you're in them. And if you're above the age of one, you've had a toxic friend. You know, the type of friend who you're always in some own sort of "Will they/Won't they" with, except instead of being unsure if you'll eventually get together, it's "Will I eventually snap and scream at them in a Macy's parking lot?" Here are some ways to spot the toxic friends in our lives:

1. **They hate everyone but you.** For years, and I do mean years, I thought I was very special because people who didn't like anyone liked me, but every time this happened, it was because this person would find one person they liked and create a toxic pattern with them, and once that person did even the smallest thing they did not like, they hated them and swiftly discarded them, to confirm their belief that everyone was bad. It's kind of the same principle as men who love that you're "not like other girls." One day you're going to land in the Other Girls pile because that's how they see the world. Side note: I love The Other Girls. The Other Girls rule. Solidarity with the Other Girls forever.

2. **You don't like the way they treat other people**. If you love the way they treat you but see them being mean to service workers, or other friends, or people who just plain aren't you, that can be a warning sign that the same path awaits you. And even if it doesn't, that might not be the kind of person you want to be friends with.

3. **You view money in totally different ways and it really stresses you out.** This is a huge one that's not spoken about often enough, and it's not about who has more money or less money, though that can absolutely impact your friendship. This one is really about the ways you're both conscious of the differing ways you view money. If they view money as not a big deal because they have a lot of it, or just don't view it as a stressor, and you view money as a

very big deal because you don't currently have a lot of it, or you grew up worrying about money, this can be a huge problem. Ideally, your friend is able to see these differences and be very mindful of them, but that's not always the case. And if it isn't, and this consistently causes friction between you too (like they know you're stressed about money and they're not and yet somehow you still have to remind them multiple times to Venmo you for dinner, which is hell) that could be a sign. Boundaries around money are still boundaries, and if they know you have them, and they're being crossed regularly, it's fair to be upset by that.

These are just a few examples I've noticed, but you don't always need a list, or for them to fit into one of these for it to feel toxic to you. Trust your intuition and that gnawing in your gut that something is off, and explore where it leads you. Once you've realized that things might be toxic, or something isn't working, and you've had the fights/productive conversations to try and rectify things (if warranted) the hardest thing can be to realize that you might actually have to leave, instead of being able to repair things and grow together. But at least you can leave knowing you did all you could to try and save it.

On Friends Leaving Without Warning

When friends leave without saying goodbye, it is a specific type of hurt and grief that we don't often speak about. The friends who left without telling you about what was wrong, even when you reached out and left the door open to talk about it because you didn't want it to end this way. That is brutal.

The important thing to remember is that when this happens, *it is usually not about you*. Yes, it would've been great if they could've told you what was wrong, but sometimes the other person left because of their own assumptions, their own fears, their own issues, or they couldn't explain what they needed and it was easier to just leave.

The other possibility is that sometimes someone did try to talk to you before they left, and didn't feel heard, so they felt they had no choice. In the past, I've had to pull away from a friend who I had tried to talk to many times about their harmful behavior—both to me and sometimes to others. It happened so often that I knew talking to them one more time was unlikely to awaken some secret other person full of compassion who was hiding under their coffee table. And I wanted to spare myself the pain of trying again and being disappointed again and maybe even spare them the pain of continually disappointing someone when they couldn't give me what I needed.

Most of the time, people who reject us and leave us out of nowhere are doing it to keep themselves safe, even if we feel like we haven't harmed them. They're doing it to avoid getting too close to people, to avoid getting hurt. Many times, people will even pat themselves on the back for this ability, for the speed and frequency with which they're able to cut and run when they decide they no longer like someone. And it's not necessarily our job to dissect that and decide if it's healthy or why they do it, even though that is often our desire.

I've also had friends who not only left out of nowhere, they turned on a dime and became vicious before they did. It was so upsetting to know they could just flip a switch, that someone I'd known as my closest friend could now become a bully, could know they're hurting me deeply and continue to do it. I can't tell you how many times that happened, especially in my teen years.

But I know from many years of reaching out to friends who had left without warning, or been cruel without warning and then left, in search of a reason they did it, this never actually gave me the closure I wanted. I would write these intensely vulnerable letters, hoping it would soften them, that they would open up and we could talk and heal it, and it never worked out that way.

So let me save you some time. If someone leaves without a word, don't chase them. Allow people who want to leave like that to leave, even if it breaks your heart more than you could ever explain.

The hardest thing to realize is that not every friendship is meant to last forever, as much as we wish it would. So many friendships are meant to show us things, good and bad, about what we want, what we need, and who we do and don't want to be, and who we do and don't want to be around.

Just because your friend left without warning doesn't mean that you are bad or that you deserve to be abandoned. And I say this as someone who has struggled with that so many times. So, hear me when I tell you: Those are not your people.

The challenging part about friendships is that both parties have to feel good about it, which is why it's critical that communication be as wide open as possible. And if you've done your best with that, and it isn't working for one of you, people are allowed to leave, even if it feels painful to us. Just as much as we are allowed to leave what isn't working, even if it feels painful to them.

Regardless of who left who, there is an unspeakable pain that is created during friendship breakups that can be just as painful as a romantic breakup, if not arguably much more so. You are grieving someone who became a part of your heart and your life and everything that makes you who you are. Someone who became your backup, someone who became your family. You had dreams of that friendship, of where it would go, what you would become. And then it just ended, and they are gone, either because they left, or you left, or they hurt you, or it just didn't work anymore, and the world tells you to just move on. Don't talk about it, bury those feelings inside you. We don't have words for this yet, we don't have a protocol, and we won't develop them until we talk about how brutal and disorienting friend breakups are.

In any of the friendships I've had to leave, even in the ones that hurt me so much, I truly hope those people have found other friendships that are a better fit for them. It's possible to end things that way, with communication, kindness, and care. It is. So if the person who left your friendship did it with unwarranted cruelty and casualty that felt like a knife in your gut, truly, that is about them. And if you're the kind of person who would never leave a friendship that was loving and kind by being cruel and casual, then why would you wanna stay friends with someone who had no problem doing that to you?

Real friends aren't also your bullies, and real friends don't stay close friends with your bullies or your abusers. So if you're seeing that happen? Well, now you have that information. And that information, even though it is shattering to have, says so much about that person and makes a great case for why you don't need them in your life, and thank goodness you realized that now.

Again, friendship is information gathering, about yourself, about the other person, and finding the things you truly want to find in the people around you. Even if it is absolutely not this person anymore. Everything they show you, everything they tell you, is a data point. An often messy, emotional data point, but a data point nonetheless. And looking at it this way often helps me take the sting out of friendship breakups that feel so achingly personal, as though the ending of this friendship had to do with your own worthiness. It does not. And realizing that has lessened the grief I've felt in my friendship breakups by miles, as well as paved the way for the next friendship, and the next.

In my experience, when you start choosing better people and start communicating better, you might realize those moments when someone hurts you, or you find you're trying to prove your worth to them, these may simply be miscommunications, or problems that are easily repairable. And on the off chance that it is not, fuck 'em. You don't want them in your life anyway.

Loyalty, in its purest sense, is not a bad thing. It can be beautiful to hold onto people tightly, to cherish them as rare gifts, yes. But we also have to remember that in many cases, taking stock of your friendships can be like cleaning out your closet. Sometimes there are people in there who used to fit us but no longer do. Or who used to make us feel good but no longer do. This doesn't mean we have to cry over it, though we can if we need to, but we can also be happy for the times when they did fit us, the times when they did make us feel good, and then remove them from your closet, and pass them along to another person who they might fit perfectly.

Similarly, maybe some friends just need new buttons or a new hem before you can wear them proudly again. And for those people, that could mean setting more boundaries, or openly communicating more of how you feel, or changing the depth at which you interact with them like we talked about in the friendship levels chapter. If you really love someone, it's worth it to see if you can make it work in a new way.

And then, if the worst-case scenario comes to fruition and the friendship ends, after you grieve it, try to let it go and remember there is now even more room in your heart for people who fit you better.

And if you're in the in-between territory of not being sure if your friendship should end, or if you should work through it, it can be helpful to remember that sometimes the best thing you can do for yourself, and for the other person, is to walk away from the friendship. Walking away can actually be an act of compassion, to release you both from the cycle of wishing you could get your friendship back to how it used to be, or what you'd hoped it would become. In the best cases, you can, grief-stricken or not, part ways resolute in the knowledge that you both really tried.

And I can promise you that both people really caring, really trying, is still a very successful friendship, even if it ends.

How Marriage and Kids Can Impact Your Friendship

We made a deal ages ago. Men, babies, it doesn't
matter. . . . We're soulmates.
> —Samantha Jones, *Sex and the City*

Years ago, I watched *Bridesmaids* and didn't fully understand why Annie was so upset that her best friend was
getting married. I didn't understand how a friend getting
married or having kids when you're not there yet or have
no desire to ever be there could feel like you were losing
someone. They're still alive and they're still your friend, so
unless they moved radically far away, I couldn't see how
coupling, marrying, or becoming a parent would change
things. Now I do.

I don't know if you can fully understand just how much
someone going through one of these life changes can shift your
friendship until it happens to you. When I saw *Bridesmaids*,
I had some friends who were married and had kids. Neither
phase of life was on my immediate radar, and I never felt
like that difference affected our friendships. How these life
changes affect your friendship often boils down to a few fac-
tors: How long had you been friends before the life change
occurred, and how close were you when it did? Did you want

to experience what they were experiencing but couldn't yet? And how did your friendship change after?

If someone gets married after you've been friends for fifteen years, it probably won't affect you as much as if you became best friends a year ago and now they're suddenly swept away by someone else. And if it does, it could have something to do with the extent to which you're feeling left out, in favor of Who The Hell Is Brad H.? And Why The Hell Does He Now Have Priority Access To My Friend? Or it might not affect you at all if that person is able to maintain their friendships and their new romantic relationships or kids, etc., without missing a beat.

I have a friend who quickly became my best friend, to the point where we both did that sweet, awkward declaration of "Are we best friends? I feel like we are!" and the other said, "OH my goodness, I was thinking that too!" and you each do a little dance in your respective hearts. We had that kind of friendship I've always wanted most, one where we text pretty much all day every day and send each other every post that makes us think of the other, which is usually every single thing we see that we love. That two halves of the same person type of friendship. And I had it! It was here! And then she met someone. And they quickly fell in love and she was with him constantly, and I had to navigate the very real conflict of "I am happy for you, and I also feel like you're gone" crossroads that can happen when one of you is going through a huge life change and the other is not. She is truly wonderful and would gladly reassure me that she was not actually gone and just caught up in this bubble, which I completely understood. And when I didn't understand it, I called my therapist. And then called my therapist again.

Even if you are over the moon for your friends when they go through these positive life changes, it is still completely normal if these shifts bring up abandonment issues, even if you know you're not actually being abandoned at all. Because for now, and maybe for now only, the friendship dynamic as you previously knew it has changed. For how long? You likely won't know. And I realized that this was yet another case of where checking in with yourself to see what you need to soothe yourself can help.

The frustrating but ultimately true fact is that after college, our life phases will directly impact our friendships in some way, large or small. And I don't directly correlate this with age, though I know many people like to. I know plenty of people in their forties who are still socially in their twenties, or people in their twenties who have old married couple energy, and both are great, so I would attribute it more to a life phase than an age range. People move, they get married, fall in love, fall in love but oops it wasn't love, find themselves, lose themselves. And friendship is about being able to love and support each other through all these phases and learning how to mold your friendship in fresh, new ways, as that clay may change and shift colors and textures into something new but not necessarily something bad. Just different.

Still, having someone go through a life change like getting married, finding a partner, or having kids, when you're personally wishing to experience that and haven't yet, can feel painful, even if you love your friend so much. As long as you're kind to this person, despite your own conflicted feelings about it, I don't believe this is a selfish way to feel. I believe it is honest. It's completely normal and reasonable to feel jealous when you see someone experiencing something you've longed for and aren't sure when it will come for you, if it will come at all.

So let's sit with that for a second. Not because there's anything wrong with being the single friend, but because society has such a complicated and strange view of "unmarried friends whose friends are already coupled or married" that people can, without even knowing, act out these subconscious (and frankly boring, deeply flawed, and often sexist) ideals, even if they know better. They are usually the following:

1. **The dreaded third-wheel hangouts.** There is a specific awkwardness that happens when you're hanging out with two people who are either all over each other in a way where you're pretty sure they forgot you're there, or having a terrible fight in front of you while you sit there eating snacks and thinking, *I guess this is how it's gonna be forever. Just me feeling like their weird child.*

2. **Getting pity invitations to things.** "We should invite Deb, don't you think? I mean she's all alone on [insert holiday or day of the week]." Then you show up and they act like they're relieved you came to their party because it means you didn't walk in front of a bus.

3. **Having to hear tons of platitudes like "You'll find someone" every time you talk to your friends.** Yes! I'm sure I will find *someone*! Finding alive people is pretty easy to do. Will I actually like them? I can't say. Will I meet them when I'm eighty-eight and have one more year of life left? Who knows? These phrases are not helping! Be specific with your fortune telling!

4. **Getting asked "Whatever happened to so and so?" like they were The One and you blew it.** "Well, I put their face on a milk carton, but thus far, no response." What do you think happened? They messed up or I messed up, but either way, something got messed up, and we're not together and it's for the best. Please never bring them up again.

5. **Watching your super-happy friends in couples being super happy.** This is wonderful on some level, it really is. And on another level, it can create anxiety if you tend to wonder if you'll ever have that, and a weird knee jerk shame can kick in that isn't your friend's fault at all, but still feels bad.

6. **Dinner parties where you're sitting in between two couples because you're the only single person there.** And if you're not the only single person there, you may be seated next to someone you would never date in a million years who thinks you're going to marry them because you're the only two single people there. How romantic! What a story to tell our children! "Well, your dad was my only option, and then we had you!"

7. **Your partnered friends may not respect your time.** These are the coupled friends who only call you when their partners are out of town. Or they assume you're never busy because you're not married or don't have children, which even if you're not busy because of that, that's a choice you were allowed to make: to not be busy in those specific ways.

8. **Your friends think all your horrible dating stories are hilarious.** "Oh goodness! You always have the wackiest

stories! Ah, to be single again. What a thrill ride." You mean going on "I wish I'd stayed home" dates that you got so excited about and then were a huge letdown, or they stopped replying, or you had to file a restraining order, all of which this chips away at your hope that love exists at all? Pass.

9. **Friends who tell you "Never get married" when they're fighting with their partner and therefore you lose all hope in love.** Don't tell me that! Tell me it's challenging, tell me it can be hard but it's worth it. But I don't want to hear "Marriage is horrible. Love is a lie" from a couple I view as a model for a relationship I'd like to have. Are you trying to kill me?

And then there's the nonstop unsolicited advice you're likely to get from people about how you're supposed to join their ranks, as happily or unhappily, as long as you're coupled. Coupled friends who give their single friends advice as though there's one way to "cure" them have got to find another way to communicate. Being the single friend is not a flaw you need to fix, it's not a problem you need to solve. And so all the platitudes of "It happens when you're not looking" or "Maybe you should just try not dating for a while" are unhelpful. No one would ever tell you this about jobs. "Oh, you can't find your dream job? Maybe you should just be unemployed for a few years even though you'll lose everything and your life will be terrible!"

We put so much pressure on one another to find the perfect partner, because everyone else around you already has, but it's interesting that we don't tend to do this with friendships. Our friends who have tight-knit friend groups don't give the same cliche advice to people who reached a certain age and still don't have their dream friends, we just sort of stop talking about it altogether. Or they try to loop you into their friend group even though it might not be the right fit for you. But that pressure for everyone to be on the same path, to reach the same milestones at certain deadlines, can still be very present. And it's just not true.

It's so easy to think we're all supposed to be on parallel tracks. That if all our friends are making these life changes at once, then they're doing everything correctly and we're failing. That they're ahead and we're behind. But the thing is, maybe all your friends who got married before you did will get divorced years later when you're getting married. Maybe the friends who had kids before you did wish they'd waited until later. Or maybe your friends who did things before you made perfect choices, and that still doesn't mean your choices are any less valid.

I know there are probably people reading this who are also struggling with being the only married friends, or the only coupled friends, or the only parent friends, who feel alienated from their friends who haven't yet hit those milestones. I've heard from many friends that they've felt very lonely when they had a new baby, and their other friends just kind of vanished because they assumed they were too busy being new parents to want to have any friends around. Which was wild to me to hear about, because that's absolutely what I'd always assumed about my friends who had kids. I didn't reach out as much because I didn't want to be the friend who doesn't have kids asking you out on a Friday night and seeming insensitive because of course you can't go or you're too tired or you need to take care of and/or want to be with your new child.

There's so much room for misunderstandings on both sides during these life changes, especially if you've never gone through that experience before. Even if you've already had kids or have gotten married before, you still may not know how your friend feels about it, or what they need from their friends now. They might still want to be invited out, even if they probably can't come, so you can compromise by asking them to come out anyway, and tell them you'll never be upset with them for saying no. This can be a great way to meet someone where they're at.

It's vital to keep the lines of communication open, with each of you prompting the other if necessary. If one of you is silently thinking, *Well I don't want to bother them because they're probably busy with their new [insert life change here]*, and the other person is thinking, *I haven't heard from them in a while, I guess they don't like me as much anymore*, what good does that do either of you?

In these cases, I think what keeps us silent, and what has kept me silent, is the fear that I am doing something wrong, expecting something unfair, or that these are just my "strange" issues, and the other person will judge me or dismiss my feelings. But when I feel like that, I have to remember that this person isn't a stranger, they are a longtime friend of mine who knows me. They probably know my issues aren't strange, but are instead very human emotions.

The fear here is usually that if you communicate those feelings they won't be able to give you what you need, or you won't see eye to eye, or you'll be judged, and there will be no way forward. But even if it can't be resolved, I've found it's always been far more worth it to attempt to resolve it, to address it head on, than to just silently wish things were different, when it might be possible that they absolutely can be. And if they can't, at least you don't have to spend any more precious energy wondering.

If your people are truly your lifelong people, they will grow with you, they will change with you, and they will honor your feelings about how they've changed, just as much as you'll honor their feelings about how you've changed. The truth is that long-term friendships will be both a grieving and discovering process throughout the years. If you can find a way to do that together, as a team, as two people who are so excited to meet every fresh self that each of you develops and blooms into, then it's absolutely worth doing.

And then you get to be eighty years old together, reflecting on all of it, in cozy wicker chairs, looking back at all the people you were throughout your lives together, grateful you both got to meet every single one.

The Frustrating Realization of the Part You Played in Choosing the Wrong Friends

I guess we all wanna be loved. It's hard to say no to
that, no matter who it's coming from.
　　　　　　　　　　　—Ruth Fisher, *Six Feet Under*

At some point in my interactions with new age hippies who
may or may not be toxic (the good ones are so good, but the
bad ones are a nightmare in yoga pants), a nightmare-in-
yoga-pants person told me that we choose everything that
will happen to us, before we are born, as part of our reincar-
nation journey.

If you just said, "Wait, what?" so did I when I heard it.
There's this idea that we chose all our traumas, heartache, and
struggles, because this was our best path to enlightenment in
this life. This is an idea I find to be deeply flawed in so many
ways, since it's far too easy to hear this and slide into a pit
called "I deserved [insert painful traumas]," that is never, ever
true. If you've attracted a nonstop stream of unhealthy friends,
I don't believe it's because you wanted unhealthy friends or
you deserved toxic friendships, but that you *tolerated* them
based on what you knew in the past, what felt familiar, and
your ability to miss or ignore red flags.

Instead of taking this as an opportunity to berate yourself and tell yourself you shouldn't be upset because you "chose" this, I view it as an opportunity to really sit with the reasons you chose people who were wrong for you, or treated you poorly, the reasons you can and can't control.

I used to spend so much of my time trying to fix the things I couldn't control, bracing myself as though I was just along for the ride in my friendships. It was only when I started addressing why I was allowing the wrong people to stay in my life that I started to realize what these often empty and poorly phrased platitudes might actually be getting at.

In all my failed friendships, I had absolutely been subconsciously drawn to people who could never really give me what I wanted or needed. I didn't know it at the time, but I had unknowingly played a role in having awful friends by tolerating incompatible behaviors that were hurting me, diminishing my own needs, and never openly confronting people to make room for change. And yes, those friends could've also initiated those conversations and many of them should've behaved better regardless, but I would often engage in friendships with people who were even less likely to be aware of these dynamics than I was at that time, let alone address them with open communication.

So I had to ask myself what it was about my beliefs about friendship that had previously caused me to pursue, or tolerate, people in these categories:

- Withholding
- Inconsistent care and affection
- Instances of emotional or even physical abuse

- Betrayal
- Inability to express emotions
- Inability to express remorse or take responsibility for their own actions
- Incapable of creating lasting change in their harmful behaviors

Similarly, I encourage you to take a moment to think back on your past friendships that ended or didn't work, or even the ones you have now that aren't working as well as you'd like, and look at what they might have in common. Feel free to use the space below to write it out.

What patterns do you tend to see in the people you're choosing to be close to? Is there anything you notice that keeps coming up for you?

_____

_____

_____

_____

_____

_____

_____

It's likely that while writing these you've already had a flash-bulb moment of "Oh my goodness, that sounds a lot like my parent, grandparent, or sibling," or someone from your childhood who was close to you. And if you haven't, you're probably having one as you read that last sentence, and that's no coincidence, but it's pretty mind-blowing how much it always comes back to that.

We often talk about how much our parents and caregivers and childhood experiences impact who we choose as a romantic partner, but we rarely if ever talk about how much we're choosing our friends in the exact same ways. So if you had very few, or zero, examples of healthy caregiving and relationships as a kid, then surprise! You have the frustrating task of realizing you might still be on autopilot when it comes to choosing, or tolerating, friends who are totally wrong for you.

Rather than remaining stuck in self-blame or shame, take pride in your ability to be honest with yourself about what led you here, that you are here, and feel the relief that you are finally seeing these patterns, and that you no longer want to repeat them. Take that information, honor it, and now use it to clear the way to getting what you really want and have—by the way—always deserved.

What to Do When You Finally Find Your People: How to Be a Good Friend

Everyone needs a friend they can call and wake up
in the middle of the night. Leslie's usually already
up . . . and often she's usually on her way over.
—Ann Perkins, *Parks and Recreation*

You'd think that by the time you find your people, you'll know
it and it will just feel great instantly and forever. But in my
experience, if you've struggled to find better friends for a long
time, you might not even notice when your friendships finally
do get better. Not because it won't be noticeable, but because
it's easy to get used to being the person who struggles with
your friendships, to get used to being disappointed, used to
being wrong about someone.

Recently I heard a friend talk about a care package her
friend sent her, and my first thought was, *Aww, I wish I had
friends who would do that for me.* A week later, a care package
from an internet friend came in the mail and it was perfect.
And I thought, *Oh wait, I have friends now kind of? I am someone who has that!?!* It felt scary and confusing, as though if I
had it now, it could also, would also, be taken away from me
just as it had been before.

Because how can you know if it's different this time?
How can you tell? We spend so much time looking for red

flags of what isn't working, what to watch out for, and how to break old patterns, but it's just as important to know how to tell when things are working. How do you know when your friendships are finally healthier, when a friendship has real promise, and when you should start trusting a friendship more because it's making you really happy? So here are the green flags:

1. **You're able to relax around them.** This is something I've consistently seen when I'm around my favorite people. And while it might take a while, especially if you have anxiety, the best people are the ones who make you feel safe to be all versions of yourself.
2. **You feel safe to make mistakes.** You feel safe to be misunderstood, safe to be given the benefit of the doubt if you say something unclear, and safe to not worry if you are doing everything "right" or else they'll be mad at you.
3. **You're able to have disagreements and communicate your feelings openly, knowing you're both on the same team.** Did I only recently realize this was possible? Yes! Did I have it in 99 percent of my past relationships? No! But this is a huge green flag, and if you have this with someone, this is such a great sign. Especially if you, like me, spent many past friendships scared to ever bring anything up. It's so freeing to be around someone who allows you to do that in a way where you know everyone will be respectful and respected.
4. **You don't worry about where you stand with them.** Or if you do, they're always quick to put you at ease and happy to address those feelings of uncertainty or insecurity that may be coming up because of your past experiences.

Which then makes it easier for you to feel that anxiety less and less until you one day you'll never feel it at all.

Sounds peaceful, right? That's the goal.

* * *

It's been surreal to occasionally realize that so many of these green flags are present in my friendships, and that I actually have friends, at least on some level. (See? I couldn't even say it definitely, that's how much anxiety I still have about it.) Friends who truly care about me and will probably stay my friends, as long as I'll let them and as long as we both maintain this living, breathing friendship we're building together.

As much as that growth feels incredible, it can still feel weirdly challenging to embrace that my story has changed and can change, and to potentially mourn the loss of my identity as someone who struggled so much with that previously, because the pain of not having it for so long and fearing I will lose it again can be so great. So if you have people in your life who you love but you struggle with those things as well, I want you to know that makes total sense to me and that you're not alone in feeling it.

The transition from "Where are my friends?" to "My friends are finally here, now what do I do?" is very real and can feel absolutely overwhelming. Part of it is addressing and mourning the loss of the part of you that became so comfortable with toxic relationships as you move into the strangely scary reality of friendships that work, friendships that are collaborative, and friendships that are still going to take some work (but at least it's not nearly as much work as your toxic friendships required). And it might not look the way you always thought it would.

My current friendships, in some ways, are absolutely what I dreamed of when I was an overly romantic teenager. And in other ways, they are very different from that ideal, as perhaps they should be. Most of our friendships won't look exactly as we'd previously thought they would, especially if our only source of how they "should" look was fictional pop culture friendships. But just because they might look different doesn't change the fact that everything we want in our friendships is still possible, even if it builds slowly, but beautifully, bit by bit throughout our lives.

Once you have friendships that feel better to you, feel promising, and seem to be off to a good start, you're now at a wonderful place where you should be mindful of three things: assessing if your friend is being a good friend to you, communicating openly to give them a chance to do better if they need to do better, and just as importantly, being a good friend to them.

For people who struggle with codependency and giving too much, the last part will be fairly innate, but since many people don't struggle with that (wow, what a gift, sounds great), this part is so important. It's so easy to become obsessed with how other people are being hurtful that sometimes we don't think about how we could be better to our friends as well. I have great compassion for this, because I know it usually comes from the fear that you don't want to get invested, or get too close to someone who you're not sure really cares about you, but that's why I keep stressing the importance of keeping both sides of this two-way street as lovely as possible.

A lot of people aren't sure what it really means to be a good friend, and a lot of it is very personal to each of us. Which is why it's a great idea to go back to the section on attachment styles and really make sure you see how it applies to you, so you can know what being a good friend looks like to each one of your friends. Ask them what their love language is! Do those things for them! Being a Good Friend is truly subjective, so showering someone with macarons every day at noon might be one person's heaven, but another person's mid-day carb-filled annoyance. (Note: if they are the latter, I will gladly take their macarons and, if I cannot finish them, keep them in my fridge to eat in about an hour. They will not go to waste either way.)

So here are some things I have learned about how to be a great friend. You don't have to do them all, and you don't have to do them all regularly, and of course they all depend on how you feel comfortable showing love. But it's nice to have a reminder of ways we can make someone feel seen, loved, and to know that we're thinking about them:

1. **If you planned on grabbing coffee, pick up coffee for both of you on the way to meet them.** I love this move so much, and we often only see it in rom-coms with cute dates, but this is such a lovely thing to do for your friends. Plus, you probably know what they were going to order anyway, and this way you're both sufficiently caffeinated for what will obviously be an incredibly charming day.

2. **Bring snacks to their place whenever you come over.** This is such a simple gesture, but it is also super sweet, especially if you both love food as much as I do. Take a moment and imagine your best friend doing this for you. You'd look at them like they were the Oprah of hangouts. *And you get a snack, and youuuuu get a snack, and youuuuuuuuuuuu get a snack!*

3. **Send them a playlist of songs that remind you of them when they're having a hard day.** It'll be much more difficult to continue beating themselves up for forgetting to do something important for their boss when they're listening to songs from their friend who was thoughtful enough to do this for them.

4. **Invite them over when you clean out your closet so they can claim any of their favorite pieces before you donate them.** It's like free shopping plus a fashion show plus donations at the end. That's a good hang out. (side note: as long as you don't TAKE THEM ALL BACK!)

5. **Sneakily tell the waiter when it's their birthday and order their favorite dessert.** So not only do they get cake, they also get an embarrassing rendition of "Happy Birthday" sung to them by a bunch of hot waiters who may not enjoy this part of their job.

6. **Write them real letters on paper with a pen.** They're not as fleeting as texts, and you can use pretty stationary. I firmly believe that everyone loves getting paper mail and that it will never go out of style.

7. **If they have you over for dinner, do the dishes without saying a word.** They might not even notice at the time, but later when they go to wash the dishes and see you already did them, they'll be like, *Aww. This is why we're friends.*

8. **Shoot them a text just to let them know you're thinking of them.** Especially if they've been stressed about something, but also just because. Who doesn't love hearing that someone is thinking of them? That's among my favorite texts to get.

9. **If you see something that you think they'd like, get it for them.** Even if it's not their birthday or Christmas or some

other gift-giving occasion. Life is short, and you somehow found each other. You can never celebrate that too much. Unless they tell you that you are, in which case stop, I guess.

If you have the sweet gestures department covered and you want to deepen what you already have, there are so many ways to do that. And even if you don't want to do anything at all, just knowing someone for years and going through all the ups and downs and changes will deepen what you have. That's the beauty of longevity and intimacy. But if you want active things you can do to bring you closer, here are some ideas.

1. **Take a really nice vacation together because you deserve it.** It doesn't have to be a five-star trip to Spain, but just taking your friends and going somewhere where there are mints on the pillows and a swim-up bar with dreamy lifeguards will make you feel like you're that group of cool best friends in the TV shows you love, which is a feeling we all deserve to have.

2. **Get to know the messiest parts of each other.** It's easy to spend a lot of your time with your friends talking about superficial things and going over the details of your day and how work was, but it's just as important to take some time to get to know the things that made them who they are. It can be so wonderful to have a whole night devoted to figuring out your friends' saddest memories, their happiest memories, their scariest memories. You do those things with people you date, so why wouldn't you do them with the friend you'll probably know for the rest of your life?

3. **Get into a massive fight and work together to move past it.** Say all the stuff you've been dying to say as directly as

possible. When I say to say it directly, I mean don't water it down in a way you're not actually communicating what's wrong, which can make it hard for the other person to help you address it. You don't want to just dump a long list of complaints on someone out of nowhere in a hurtful way, but you do want to be honest about painful things in a way that lets the other person know what you need and how you feel. Because once you purge all of that from your relationship, you'll not only be rid of all that hidden baggage between you, it'll show you that your friendship is strong as hell and can handle even the worst of fights, which is actually super comforting. And if you need a reminder of how to fight in a better way, you can revisit the chapter in here about that.

One of the biggest things I've had to remind myself is that friendships don't have to look a certain way for them to "count." And if you've had a hard time feeling safe around people, it might take you years to really feel like you do have friends, and something horrible won't come along to wash it all away.

I've also realized that every time I've thought something was missing from a friendship, or something was off, this was a reminder to address my own boundaries again. This comes up for me often, and if it comes up for you often, you can go back to those sections of the book again and again. If you feel confused about your own feelings, or when and how to address problems in your friendship, this book is meant to be used over and over again to support you. Even if things have been great with you and your friend for years, you still might once again find things are off-kilter, or realize you no longer make each other happy, and you need to ask yourself why, and then decide what to do. That's a great time to go back through those sections, bookmark them feverishly, and remind yourself there are tools and these feelings of discomfort are not permanent. There is always a solution, even when it feels like there isn't.

As much as I might want to just bail on a friendship that has been fraying, I remind myself to use these moments as powerful opportunities to be mindful of my own needs and boundaries and how openly and effectively I can communicate them. Even if it doesn't repair this particular friendship, this is an invaluable skill that will still carry you into the next friendship, and the next after that.

And if you're not able to get there in your friendships yet, that is OK. If you made some great progress, but still have wounds to heal around this topic, that is OK. If you're still waiting to find your people or aren't sure if you've found them or not, that is OK. And if you've realized you have found your people and now know how to have a better relationship with them, or you're still waiting to meet your people but now you are fully prepared to meet them and excited to experience friendships you've always wanted, I am so glad.

Above all, it's OK if you still want the fictional friendships you saw growing up, while also remembering that those friendships, while comforting, are not always realistic, and comparing our real-life friendships to them can quickly become an exercise in masochism.

So it becomes a balancing act between not settling and realizing that real-life friendships are textured and can change shape and quite possibly become as close to what you'd always hoped for through communication and boundaries. Many of us love TV "hangout shows," because watching people have great friendships on TV is so much less complicated than navigating our friendships in real life. But I know it is worth it for those moments when your friendship not only feels as good as the friendships you see on TV, it feels even better because it's real.

I've started to realize that maybe I *did* find my people, and maybe the people I've been waiting for and romanticized meeting are already around me, even if it's only one or two people. Maybe so much about finding your people is realizing when you've found them. Because if you have someone who's willing to work on your friendship with you, even if it doesn't look like you'd hoped, but it's very close, then maybe you can get it to that place together. As much as it might seem like finding your people will be a watershed moment when you step into a new reality and dust yourself off, thinking, *That's settled, onto the next wonderful phase*, it's possible there will be a surprising grieving process involved.

As I've realized more and more that I have found my people, at least some of them, I've had to work to grieve and release the part of me that didn't think it could happen, is still hurting from all the friendships that were harmful or that I lost, and is still scared my new friendships will go away or become harmful. It's weirdly hard to let go of that identity, even though it was uncomfortable. It's so easy to turn something you didn't want (to not have your people) into an identity, as a way to cope with the pain. "I don't have the friends I want, but it's fine, I'm a cool loner, it's actually a badge of coolness." And then one day you finally think you've found your people, but then they hurt you, or it falls apart, and you're once again back to what you knew: solitude, disappointment, loneliness, and the want for something better.

Often when you finally see some consistency, healing, and improvement, it's likely you'll still cycle through those abandonment fears, and maybe even a total dismissal of these people as real friends, because some part of you got so used to the feeling of waiting for them. We feel safest with what we know. You know how to deal with wanting more from people, you know how to fantasize about what your perfect friends will be like one day, so then when you get closer to having them, or even finally have them, that can feel terrifying. You're new to feeling this positively about your friendships, so how will you handle it? And what if you feel like you've found your people to some extent, but you still hope for even more, from them or someone else?

Finding your people is all of these things. It's grief, and hope, and fear, and work, and adjustment and communication. It's easy and it's hard, it's confronting past wounds and making room in your heart and your brain to accept that things could be better now, are better now. Even if it's not exactly perfect yet. Even if the perfect friendship, as you'd grown up defining it, doesn't exist, or has changed its meaning entirely. Some part of finding your people is really about enjoying whatever path you're on and reveling in any and all moments of joy and connection that will lead you to the purely good friendships you're meant to have. Maybe it's the friends you have now, maybe it's not. But there's good to be found in them all, and there are lessons in every one of them that will take you to where you want to go.

And I want you to have that unshakeable faith in yourself, that you will find the friendships you dream of, and you will get everything you want in them, even the biggest friendship dreams you never told anyone about.

Some people have always fantasized about their wedding day. They dream of what their outfit will be like, what the music will be, the kinds of flowers they'd choose, seeing all the people they love there to celebrate them. Why is marriage the only thing we fantasize when it comes to our relationships? Because

I can tell you right now, when I think about the best-case scenario of how it will be when I find my people, I can see it all just as clearly.

What would it look like to you, to finally have the friendships you dreamed of as a child, or even dream of now? Maybe it's having the ultimate copilot on a really incredible road trip overseas for two months. Or maybe it's finally having an emergency contact you can write down without even thinking about it, someone you know who will always be there if you need them. For me, I always think of having a surprise party.

I have thrown surprise parties for other people, and attended many, but I have never had one (yet, still hopeful). To me, a surprise party is the dreamiest final form of friendship and I want it so very much. I've wanted one since I was a little kid, and with every year since, I want one even more.

I want a surprise fucking birthday party thrown by my friends that I didn't have to do anything to organize. I want everyone I love to be there, and I want fucking gifts. I want to open those gifts and not think for a second about what I have to do to pay them back, or if I deserve them, or about all of the birthdays I spent without any gifts at all. I want to walk through that door and step into a world where I am known, where I am seen, where I am celebrated. I want lights and I want a great playlist I didn't have to make myself but is just as good as if I had. I want all my favorite foods to be there, and then another secret plate of food that's in the back just for me after the party. I want the air to feel good. I want to know this party is for me, for all the things I've been and all that I'm becoming. And I want to enjoy it, not as my past self who didn't get this or my future self looking back at it, but as the person I am in this moment, feeling as loved as I should've always been.

I want to know, with every bone in my body, that it was a gift for my friends to be able to do this for me, that it was not done out of obligation or for someone else's selfish reasons, or to serve someone's ego. I am not a shelter cat, no one ever is. I know that people are, no matter what has chipped away at them, deserving of love and boundless adoration. And if it took so long to get here? That's OK. Some people don't meet their soulmates until they're sixty, but they deserved that love every day prior, just the same.

I want that birthday party and the next. I want a party for all the years no one threw me one, and for all the pitiful celebrations I threw for myself that would bum you out if you saw them in a movie. I want what everyone else seemingly gets. And if that means letting go of the disappointing friendships that I keep trying to solve like a Rubik's Cube and taking that terrifying leap into a new world where I, once again, have no one, then count me in.

I'll start over a thousand times if that's what it takes, like it's the first day at a new school, but the people here are better and closer to what I want and, hell, might even be exactly what I want. I'm willing to be scared. I'm willing to find out.

If the friends I'm meant to have are out there, just on the other side of this all-encompassing fear, waiting for me to meet them, then I want to do it. Is it fair to have to keep starting over? Should we have to cross this bridge for the ninetieth time to find what some people have their whole lives? Maybe not. Probably not. But if it's between being angry that it isn't fair— that it should've happened sooner and easier—and just getting the hell over to the other side? I'd rather be over there.

I want my fucking birthday party. And I want you to have yours too. I have faith you will arrive there, at the most perfect moment.

LANE MOORE is an award-winning comedian, actor, writer, and musician. She is the creator of the hit comedy show Tinder Live and author of the critically acclaimed book *How to Be Alone: If You Want To, and Even If You Don't*. Moore is the front person and songwriter in the band It Was Romance, which has been praised everywhere from *Pitchfork* to *Vogue*. She has written for *The Onion*, *The New Yorker*, and was previously the Sex and Relationships editor at *Cosmopolitan*. You can follow Lane at @HelloLaneMoore and LaneMoore.org.